MODEL RAILWAY CONSTRUCTOR PLANBOOK 1

BULLEID COACHES IN 4mm SCALE

S.W.STEVENS-STRATTEN

LONDON

IAN ALLAN LTD

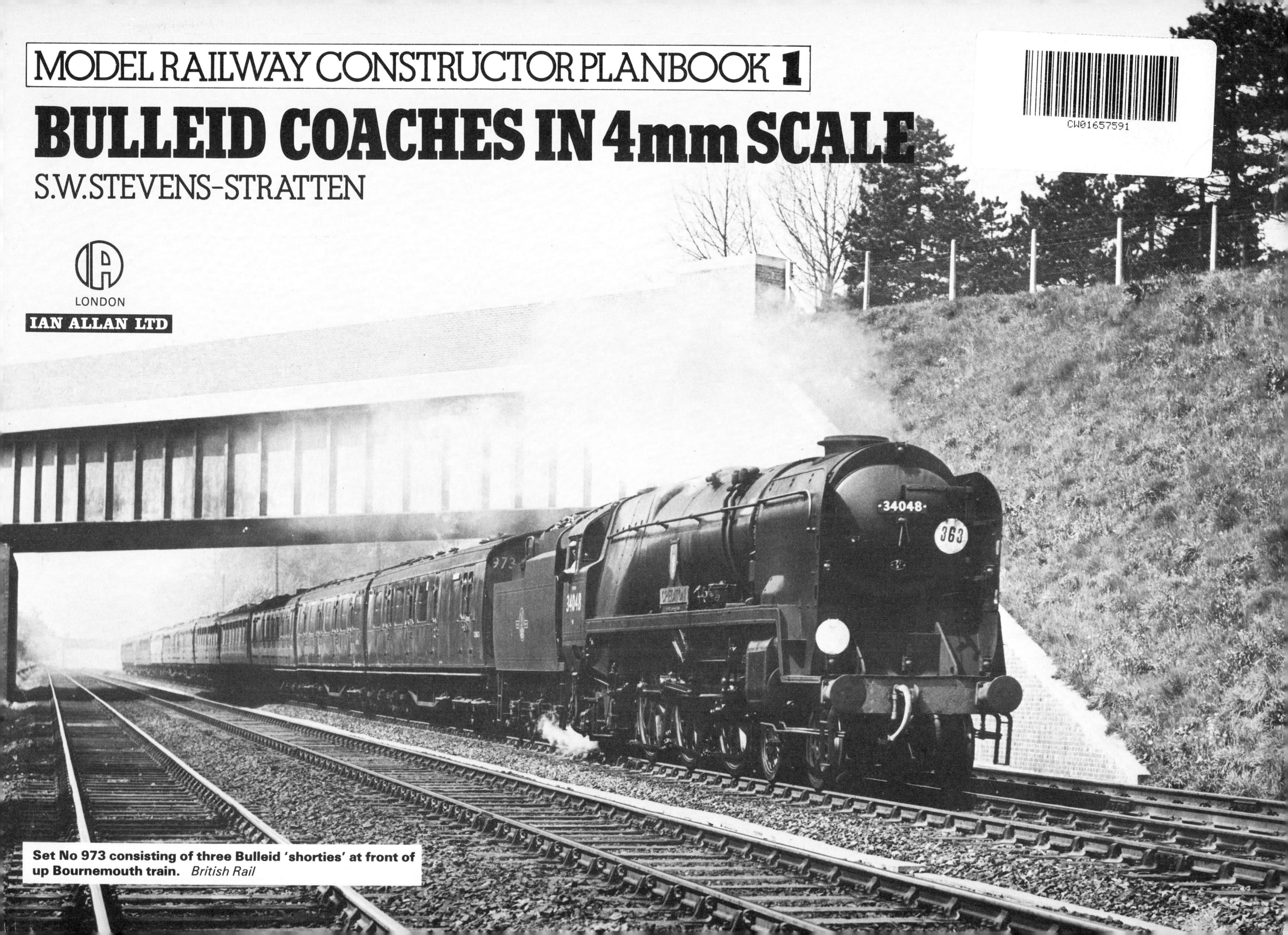

Set No 973 consisting of three Bulleid 'shorties' at front of up Bournemouth train. *British Rail*

First published 1983

ISBN 0 7110 1329 2

Published by Ian Allan Ltd, Shepperton, Surrey; and printed by Ian Allan Printing Ltd at their works at Coombelands in Runnymede, England

Front cover, left: **A Bulleid designed 4SUB emu approaches West Ewell station on a Waterloo-Epsom train in 1968.** *S. W. Stevens-Stratten*

Front cover, right: **A Corridor Composite coach from one of the original three coach sets, but now preserved on the Bluebell Railway and shown here at Sheffield Park.** *M. Harris*

Bulleid 'Shortie' 59ft corridor brake third the last coach of a train being banked up the gradient at Upwey Wishing Well in June 1967. *Brian Stephenson*

Contents

An Open saloon third for 'loose' working being shunted at Clapham Junction. *G. M. Kichenside*

Introduction

On 31 October 1937 Richard Edward Lloyd Maunsell, then aged 69 and in failing health, retired from the position of Chief Mechanical Engineer of the Southern Railway. At the instigation of Sir Herbert Walker, the General Manager and Sir Robert Holland-Martin, the Chairman it was decided that the replacement should be Oliver Vaughan Bulleid. The new CME had considerable experience of coaching stock on the Great Northern Railway from 1919-23 as Manager of the Carriage & Wagon Works at Doncaster and, of course, he was well versed in locomotive matters as Principal Assistant to Sir Nigel Gresley on the LNER.

For some time before the appointment of the new CME, the General Manager and other members of the Southern Railway Board were conscious of the fact that apart from their new electrified main line services (Brighton, Worthing, Eastbourne and Portsmouth), their steam hauled coaches were below the standard provided by the other three main railway companies. Thus Bulleid put his talents into the design of new coaching stock and his first contribution was in 1938 with the Buffet cars for the 4BUF electric sets for the Victoria-Bognor-Portsmouth services. The interior design was clean and comfortable, so much so that passengers did not want to vacate their seats and lingered too long over their snacks and drinks, thus stopping the flow of fresh customers and losing profits.

In 1938 Bulleid, assisted by L. Lynes, Technical Assistant (Carriages and Wagons) started designs for new steam hauled stock for the Bournemouth and Weymouth services. An order was placed on Lancing Works for the supply of 54 underframes of 57ft 11in length plus the normal bogies. These were completed in 1940 but prior to the final delivery a wartime prohibition on the construction of new bodywork was in force. It was therefore September 1944 before 66 new bodies could be ordered, 54 of them using the completed but stored underframes. Fourteen months later the first 59ft long coaches (61ft 7in over buffers) were finished at Eastleigh. These coaches although obviously new and bearing the now familiar Bulleid hallmark of a continuous curved bodyside with small fixed windows above the main door windows, still exhibited Maunsell styling particularly as regards the interior decor. The coaches were a composite with four 1st and three 3rd class compartments (Nos 5709-26) and a brake third with five compartments of four-aside seating plus a large (22ft long) brake van (Nos 2841-76).

The first of the real Bulleid coaches was completed in mid-1945 when it was exhibited at London termini for public reaction. No 5751 was a composite with four 1st and three 3rd class compartments plus two toilets. It was the longest coach the Southern had ever built being on a 63ft 5in underframe, it was 64ft 6in long over end panels and 67ft 1in over buffers. It was 3in wider than existing stock internally, but the same overall width and the same weight as prewar coaches (approx 34ton tare). It was revolutionary with a curved bodyside giving a bulge above the waistline (at shoulder height for seated passengers) just where extra width was needed — the same as the 4SUB electric sets already introduced. There were doors only at the ends and in the middle of the coach — no longer a case of every compartment having its own door. Thus with large windows and sliding ventilator type windows above it was an all steel shell devoid of panels, a clean and almost 'streamlined' appearance was obtained.

The interiors had hammock seating frames in which loose spring insert cushions were fitted, thus giving an unobtructive space under the seats — a big aid for cleaning. Diffused lighting in compartments which, apart from the prototype, also had individual reading lights. Electrically heated panels under the floor mats for keeping passengers' feet warm at just below blood temperature were also fitted, the current being derived from axle driven generators at 230V. In addition the normal type of steam heating was also employed. The former underfloor heating was changed when the full production coaches were built. Stainless steel was used for all fittings and there was liberal use of polished veneers for panelling and side wall coverings. Deep green sunblinds were recessed in the pelmet above all windows. Ceilings were plywood, painted gloss white and included a ventilator, plus a naked electric light bulb in a metal reflector.

The three-aside seating in the first class compartments was provided by deep individual cushions covered in deep green tapestry (moquette), with a cream and heather floral motif patterning, which blended well with the polished walnut woodwork. Armrests were also fitted between each seat.

The four-aside seating in the third class was basically a rust-brown moquette with a floral pattern but no individual armrests, only those at the end of the row of seats against the side having such luxury. The wood veneer panelling was a light mahogany. Ventilation was provided by an air duct in the upper part of the corridor partition with roof torpedo extractors. Corridor doors had interlocking brushes to prevent draughts.

Toilets were redesigned with a waterseal WC pedestal with a valve which released a measured amount of water for flushing. Rectangular handbasins had hot and cold taps, the former being fed from an electrically heated boiler, but this was later removed as it proved troublesome in service.

During the public preview over 25,000 people inspected the coach and it is significant that in the final analysis three to one were in favour of compartment type coaches as against the open saloon type. This consensus of opinion was reversed within a few years when vandalism and 'mugging' attacks came to the forefront. Many useful comments were made and some of the opinions were incorporated into the production stock.

Contrary to views often expressed the locomotive hauled coaches had hardwood framing mostly 2in square section (in the last types built from 1950 this was increased to $2\frac{1}{2}$in). This body frame was bolted on to a steel section which was welded on to the underframe. The roof was wooden boards covered with canvas. The reason for wood framing was due to the variations in design of the various types of coach and it would not have been practical to have vary large jigs to 'mass-produce' long sections which could have been common of all types. The hardwood framing was mainly vertical pillars which were thicker and closer together at points of major stress and, of course, at corners, etc. Horizontal stringers were joined to the verticals. All joints were mortised and tenoned although some were half-lapped. The steel plates were bolted to this framing and butt-welded at the joints which were then covered with a strip of metal screwed through to the wood.

The floor was layers of softwood up to $1\frac{1}{2}$in thick covered with hardboard and linoleum. There was a small sunken well, almost the depth of the floor, at each doorway to take a foot mat, but it was found that this was the cause of rotting of both wood and steel and these were later discarded and replaced with traditional flooring. The framing for all the doors was pressed steel and of similar pattern to the 4SUB electric units.

The underframes were of normal riveted steel construction (Eastleigh did not undertake welded underframes until the construction of the BR standard stock in 1951/2). The standard Southern Railway pattern 8ft wheelbase bogie was fitted also the standard Southern type of gangway based on the Pullman pattern.

The Bulleid coaches most certainly put the Southern on the map as far as coaching stock and comfort were concerned, built when there was an urgent need for new stock with a general shortage of materials following the aftermath of the war and with little time for experiments. Generally speaking they gave yeoman service with intensive use. Admittedly faults did develop, and it was not unknown for body panelling to work loose and for the butt welded joints to sometimes split which caused rusting to commence. However, it was usually about 12 years before major repairs and recladding had to be undertaken, and this was not a difficult task for works such as Eastleigh.

Acknowledgement must be made to 'VE', F. Robertson and R. H. Fielding who produced the drawings and to Graham Burtenshaw and Michael Welch whose articles in the August and October '79 issues of *Railway World* provided some of the data. Also Jane Quenault for redrawing the EMU stock.

Livery

All the Bulleid stock built during the regime of the former Southern Railway was painted in their standard colour of Malachite green (officially known as New green No 3). There was no lining on the coach sides; the lettering and numerals were the 'Sunshine' style adopted by the SR using golden yellow paint shaded black in the positions shown on the respective drawings. At first the class numerals ('1' and '3') were shown on the respective carriage doors, but when 3rd class became 2nd class, only the first class sections were shown. Later this was augmented by the yellow band at cant rail level.

After Nationalisation the coach numbers were prefixed by an 'S' and were gradually changed to a BR style of Gill Sans numerals in a golden colour with black edging. These numbers were placed at the left hand end at waist height, but changed in 1951 to the right hand end of both sides of the coach.

The roofs of the coaches were mid-grey (when new), the underframes were black as were the coach ends, but the six-coach sets for the Bournemouth line had green ends with the set number in yellow.

After nationalisation six-coach set No 299 and three-coach set No 788 were painted in the experimental livery of plum and spilt milk (which after a period of time gave the impression that the fruit had ripened and the milk had soured). Later when BR had settled on their crimson and cream (or blood and custard) colours, many of the Bulleid sets appeared in this livery, although the Southern Region never appeared to have as many coaches painted in these colours as some other regions, and they very quickly reverted to their green (not malachite) when they were allowed some autonomy.

The Bulleid coaches which were sent to other regions were usually painted in the all-over maroon livery, but some were later put into the blue and grey livery.

Notes for Modellers

While coach numbers are given it must be remembered that vehicles did change around in sets, particularly in the later days. The information as printed is correct for the earlier days. Withdrawal dates are given as these may be helpful in assessing the period when a particular coach was in service.

At the time of writing there have been no proprietary models of Bulleid coaches, with the exception of the three produced by Fleischmann in 3.5mm (HO) scale. Airfix, before their financial collapse and subsequent take-over by Mainline (Palitoy) had announced that Bulleid coaches would be available by 1982, but we now understand that no tooling up had been undertaken.

The situation is better as regards to kits and there is a large range in 4mm from Phoenix Coach Kits (originally named BSL) and marketed by Hobbytime (5 and 7 Ravenswood Crescent, West Wickham, Kent) and some electric units from Modern Traction Kits (60 Queens Street, Maidenhead, Berks). In 7mm scale (O gauge) complete kits are available from Postwar Prototypes (12 Delisle Road, Winton, Bournemouth, Dorset) and body shell kits from Westdale Coaches and Models (32 Ashley Gardens, Waltham Chase, Southampton). In gauge 1 there are kits from Tenmille Products (Station Road, East Preston, Littlehampton, Sussex).

The bogie carrying one end of coach No 5716 — a corridor composite, which is being propelled through the carriage washing plant at Clapham Junction. *British Rail*

Interior of the saloon section in the Corridor dining first. Note the fluorescent lighting in the ceiling and normal tungsten lamps in the table lights. *British Rail*

Coach Numbers and Formations

Type of coach	*Drg No*	*Coach Nos*	*Window vents (inch)*	*Water tank*	*Steps*
6 Coach sets Nos 290-300					
Semi-open brake third	3	4349-4369	10¼	Short	Short
Corridor composite	4	5740-5750	10¼	Short	Short
Corridor dining first	5	7677-7687	10¼	Short	Short
Kitchen & Dining third	6	7881-7891	10¼	Short	Short
Open saloon third	7	1451-1461	10¼	Long	Short
Semi-open brake third	3	4350-4370	10¼	Short	Short
5 Coach sets Nos 830-849					
Semi-open brake third	9	3971-4009	15	Short	Short
Corridor third	13	41-79	15	Long	Short
Corridor composite	10	5848-5867	15	Short	Short
Corridor third	13	42-80	15	Long	Short
Semi-open brake third	9	3972-4010	15	Short	Short
4 Coach sets Nos 80-94					
Semi-open brake third	9	4011-4039	15	Short	Short
Corridor composite	10	5823-5837	15	Short	Short
Corridor third	13	26-40	15	Long	Short
Semi-open brake third	9	4012-4040	15	Short	Short
3 Coach sets Nos 770-793					
Semi-open brake third	9	4301-4347	10¼	Short	Long
Corridor composite	10	5751-5774	10¼	Short	Long
Semi-open brake third	9	4302-4348	10¼	Short	Long
3 Coach sets Nos 850-865 (Slightly different underframe)					
Semi-open brake third	9	2501-2531	15	Long	Short
Corridor composite	10	5908-5923	15	Long	Short
Semi-open brake third	9	2502-2532	15	Long	Short
3 Coach sets Nos 795-804 (Built by BRCW)					
Semi-open brake third	21	4209-4227	10¼	Short	
Corridor composite	19	5775-5784			
Semi-open brake third	21	4210-4228			

Type of coach	*Drg No*	*Coach Nos*	*Window vents (inch)*	*Water tank*	*Steps*
3 Coach set No 805 (Built by BRCW)					
Semi-open brake third	20	4229	10¼	Short	Long
Corridor composite		5785	10¼	Short	Long
Semi-open brake third	20	4320	10¼	Short	Long
3 Coach set Nos 806-818 (Built by BRCW)					
Semi-open brake third	20	4251-4275	10¼	Short	Long
Corridor composite	19	5786-5798	10¼	Short	Long
Semi-open brake third	20	4252-4276	10¼	Short	Long
3 Coach set Nos 819-829 (Built by BRCW)					
Semi-open brake third	20	4277-4297	10¼	Short	Long
Corridor composite	19	5812-5822	10¼	Short	Long
Semi-open brake third	20	4278-4298	10¼	Short	Long
3 Coach sets Nos 981-984 (63ft 5in early design)					
Semi-open brake third	15	2877-2883	10¼	Short	Long
Corridor composite	16	5720-5730	10¼	Short	Long
Semi-open brake third	15	2878-2884	10¼	Short	Long
3 Coach sets Nos 963-980 (59ft)					
Semi-open brake third	17	2841-2875		Short	
Corridor composite	18	5709-5726		Short	
Semi-open brake third	17	2842-2876		Short	
2 Coach set Nos 63-75					
Semi-open brake third	9		10¼	Short	
Brake composite	11	6700-6712	10¼		
3 Coach set 767-769 (new set from 'loose' vehicles)					
Semi-open brake third		3950-3955			
Corridor composite		5878-5880			

The above is the situation when the coaches were new, but they soon changed around due to damage, repairs and maintenance, then coaches were substituted for 'loose' vehicles.

Many five-coach sets (Nos 830-849) were reduced to three-coach sets by removing the two corridor thirds, which were put into the 'pool' of 'loose' vehicles. Some of the three-coach sets (Nos 850-865) have been augmented by two 'loose' corridor thirds (from Nos 81 upwards) to form a five-coach set. Sets Nos 263-267 had various formations for 6-10 vehicles, brake thirds, composites and corridor thirds.

Sets Nos 350-356 were often used for Ocean Liner Boat trains.

Reference to numbers shown on drawings, where applicable

1 Standard type Southern torpedo ventilator.
2 Combined door top light and ventilator.
3 End step and bracket fixed to underframe.
4 Lower step and bracket fixed to underframe.
5 Guard's lookout periscope.
6 Southern standard 10$\frac{1}{4}$in high sliding window ventilator.
6A British Rail standard 15in high sliding window ventilator.
7 Mushroom type lavatory ventilator.
8 Lavatory window with 10$\frac{1}{4}$in high ventilator SR type.
8A Lavatory window with 15in high ventilator BR type.
9 Water tank top and filler.
10 Brackets for roof destination boards.
11 Passenger emergency brake application cock and operating gear.
12 Water tank filler nozzles.
13 Third class compartment seating (dotted).
14 Third class saloon seating (dotted).
15 Brackets for reservation (etc) boards.
16 Handrail (for step ends).
17 Handbrake column and wheel for guard.
18 Reservation board.
19 Destination board (small).
20 Roof destination board.
21 Corridor handrails (inside windows).
22 Handrail and tank filler pipe.
23 First class compartment seating (dotted).
24 First class dining saloon chairs (dotted).
25 First class dining saloon tables and lamps (dotted).
26 Dining saloon curtains.
27 Third class dining saloon chairs (dotted).
28 Third class dining saloon tables and lamps (dotted).
29 Extractor propeller fans.
30 Kitchen cooking range ventilator.
31 Lighting control 'jumper' cables.
32 Lamp 'irons' or brackets.
33 Lamp iron secured to footstep.
34 Handrail.
35 Coach end footstep.
36 Builders weight and dimension plates.
37 Long stepboard across two of item 35.
38 Set number (painted on).
39 Flexible vestibule connection — Pullman type.
40 Filler pipe support bracket.
41 Expanded metal screen for luggage.
42 Door hinge — Three off per door.
43 Door stops.
44 Door handles.
45 Commode handles.
46 Rainstrips on roof.
47 Cornice of 'cant' strip.
48 'Monsoon' ventilators.

◀ **A six-coach set (No 290) for the Bournemouth services. The distinguishing feature is the body sides extended over the solebars. A semi-open brake third is at each end of the rake.** *British Rail*

▼ **One of the three-coach sets (No 771).** *British Rail*

Steam hauled stock

Underframes and bogies — Drawing No 1

The underframe shown here is for all coaches from the second batch built in 1945. It is 63ft 5in long, giving an overall coach length of 67ft 1in. Note these underframes should *not* be used for the first batch of three-coach sets Nos 963-980 incorporating the brake thirds Nos 2841-2876 and composites Nos 5709-5726 as these were shorter coaches. (58ft underframe giving overall length (buffers extended) of 61ft 7in.)

There were many detail changes in the underframes, for example the early three-coach sets in the 770 series had a different equipment layout from those of the later series. The former had the usual two sets of brakegear and two vacuum reservoirs, the latter had one large brake cylinder placed amidships and one large vacuum cylinder. In more recent years many reverted to the style of the earlier series, but the single reservoir has been left intact except on the Restaurant thirds of the Bournemouth six-coach rakes.

All the underframes were riveted mild steel and were not welded as many people seem to imagine.

The drawing of the bogie represents the standard type of SR steam hauled coach bogie.

Semi-open Brake Third — Drawing No 3

These coaches were designed for the six-coach sets for the Bournemouth trains and therefore had the extended skirt (or the body side being continued down over the solebars). They also had the small and separate stepboards and the smaller ($10\frac{1}{4}$in) sliding ventilators above the main windows.

The coaches are virtually the same as those constructed for 'loose' working (see drawing No 7).

Coach Nos: 4301-4383
Diagram: 2123
Built: 11/46
Withdrawn: All by 12/67
Seating: 2×3rd with 8 seats
Saloon with 32 seats
Notes: 4349-4370 allocated to set Nos 290-300

Corridor Composite — Drawing No 4

Used in the six-coach sets for the Bournemouth trains (Sets Nos 290-300) these coaches had the extended side panels and the $10\frac{1}{4}$in deep sliding window vents and the short water tanks, which was the case with all coaches up to No 5811.

The coaches were extensively used as 'loose vehicles' and proved most useful to the operating staff.

Coach Nos: 5740-5750
Diagram: 2318
Built: 12/46-5/51
Withdrawn: 4/52-11/68
Seating: 4×1st with 6 seats
3×3rd with 8 seats
Notes: Nos 5740-5750 in sets Nos 290-300

Corridor Dining First — Drawing No 5

Bournemouth line and had the sides extended down to the bottom of the solebar with the narrower sliding window ventilators, also the shorter water tanks and the short stepboards. The underframes had only one set of brakegear. The coaches were matching the third class kitchen cars Nos 7881-7891 and ran with the dining saloon adjoining the kitchen end of the third class coach. The corridor dining first was unusual as it was compartment and saloon in the same vehicle.

The interior of the compartments was panelled with satinwood with silver greywood banding while the seats were covered with uncut green moquette. The saloon had sides covered in off-white rexine and green silk curtains and maroon carpet. These coaches were the first to have fluorescent lighting tubes although normal tungten bulbs were supplied for the table lights.

Coach Nos: 7677-7687
Diagram: 2507
Built: 8/47-3/48
Withdrawn: 12/63-8/67
Seating: 3×1st with 6 seats
Saloon with 24 seats
Notes: In set Nos 290-300

Semi-open brake third No 4350 in Bournemouth six-coach set. *S. Creer*

Kitchen and Dining Third — Drawing No 6

Built for the Bournemouth six-coach sets and thus had the extended sides and the narrow sliding window ventilators they were coupled to the Corridor Dining first so that the kitchen end of this coach was next to the dining saloon of the other vehicle (drawing No 5).

Outside contractors supplied and installed all the cooking equipment. The floor of the kitchen section was covered with stone coloured tiles, while the walls and ceilings were a Holoplast panelling.

The interior of the saloon was Nigerian walnut with a different wood banding and the corridor sides were mahogany. The chairs were walnut with rust brown moquette seat coverings.

Coach Nos: 7881-7891
Diagram: 2660
Built: 8/47-3/48
Withdrawn: 2/63-8/65
Seating: Saloon with 32 seats
Notes: In set Nos 290-300

These coaches were first designated RU then RKT and finally RKS.

Open Saloon Third — Drawing No 7

These coaches have the extended sides for the six coach sets for the Bournemouth line services, but otherwise are the same as those built for loose working — see drawing No 13.

Coach Nos: 1451-1460
Diagram: 2017
Built: 8/47-1/51
Withdrawn: 1/65-11/68
Seating: 2 saloons of 32 seats
Notes: Allocated to sets Nos 290-300

◀ **Interior views of the kitchen section of the Kitchen and Dining third.** *British Rail*

▲ **Interior view of third class restaurant car showing glass top tables and loose chairs.** *British Rail*

▼ **Interior of open saloon third. Interior is the same as similar 'loose' coaches shown in drawing No 14.** *British Rail*

▼ **Open saloon third No 1451. As this is one of the Bournemouth six-coach sets it has the extended sides but is otherwise the same as those used on 'loose' workings.** *T. C. Robbins*

Semi-open Brake Third — Drawing No 8

These vehicles were the most numerous of the Bulleid coaches, being built in batches from 1946-51. They were originally coupled to each end of the three-, four- and five-coach sets and formed one of the vehicles in the two-coach sets.

There was some variation in the depth of the sliding window ventilators as these had the 10¼in type on some in the three and two coach rakes. There were also variations in the length of stepboards and watertanks. Another variation appears in the wire mesh grille separating the luggage compartment from the corridor as the earlier versions were of solid partitions.

◄ **Semi-open brake third No 4342, originally in three coach set No 77.** *T. C. Robbins*

▲ **The corridor side of a corridor third coach.** *T. C. Robbins*

Coach Nos:	2501-2532	3943-3962	3971-4040	4301-4348	4371-4383
Diagram:	2123	2123	2123	2123	2123
Built:	1/51-6/51	9/49-11/49	12/48-7/50	11/46-12/47	11/46-12/47
Withdrawn:	4/64-11/67	5/64-12/67	4/64-12/67	4/64-12/67	4/64-12/67
Seating:	2×3rd with 8 seats Saloon with 32 seats	2×3rd with 8 seats Saloon with 32 seats	2×3rd with 8 seats Saloon with 32 seats	2×3rd with 8 seats Saloon with 32 seats	2×3rd with 8 seats Saloon with 32 seats
Notes:	Set Nos 850-865	Loose vehicles	3971-4010 in set Nos 830-849 4011-4040 in set Nos 80-94	Set Nos 770-793	Set Nos 63-75

No 2515 has been restored and is on the Bluebell Railway.
No 4365 is being restored and will be used on the Swanage Railway.

Corridor Third — Drawing No 9

These vehicles followed the design of other coaches with no special peculiarities, and they were exchanged around considerably, particularly in the later years. An almost identical layout exists with the standard British Rail SK coaches.

Coach Nos: 12-130
Diagram: 2019
Built: 12/48-11/50
Withdrawn: 5/64-12/67
Seating: 8×3rd with 8 seats
Notes: 24-40 in set Nos 80-94
41-80 in set Nos 830-849
81-130 loose

◄ **The compartment side of a corridor third coach No 55.** *G. M. Kichenside*

▼ **The compartment side of corridor composite No 5751 as built. Note the position of class classification numerals, etc.** *British Rail*

Corridor Composite — Drawing No 10

These coaches were identical with those for the Bournemouth trains (drawing No 4) except they did not have the extended side panels, etc. These coaches were extensively used as 'loose vehicles' and proved most useful for the operating staff.

Coach Nos:	5751-5774	5799-5811	5823-5837	5848-5923
Diagram:	2318	2318	2318	2318
Notes:	Set Nos 770-793	Loose	Set Nos 80-94	5848-5867 in set Nos 830-849 5868-5907 loose* 5908-5923 in set Nos 850-849

* Different underframe.
No 5898 written off in accident.

Brake Composite — Drawing No 11

Designed specifically for use with the Semi-open brake third to form a self contained two-coach set for the routes in the West of England. These units were detached from the main line train from Waterloo at a junction station and then proceeded down the branch — very often hauled by a Class M7 0-4-4T. The town using two-coach trains were, among others, Seaton, Sidmouth, Torrington, Bude, Padstow and Ilfracombe.

Coach Nos: 6700-6712
Diagram: 2405
Built: 3/48-6/48
Withdrawn: 5/64-11/67
Seating: 2×1st with 6 seats
4×3rd with 8 seats
Notes: In set Nos 63-75

Brake Composite — Drawing No 12

Designed for loose working and usually coupled with open third saloons, these coaches are similar to the brake composite Nos 6700-6712 (drawing No 11), but the toilet compartment is moved to the centre of the coach. All these vehicles had the shallow type window ventilators.

Coach Nos: 6713-6752
Diagram: 2406
Built: 6/48-9/48
Withdrawn: 4/64-9/68
Seating: 2×1st with 6 seats
4×3rd with 8 seats

The corridor side of a 'loose' brake composite No 6741.
T. C. Robbins

Corridor First — Drawing No 13

These coaches were originally intended as 'loose vehicles' to be formed into continental boat trains and ocean liner express trains as required. In later years many found their way into permanent or semi-permanent rakes of coaches on a wide variety of duties.

These vehicles were never in pure Southern livery or with Southern lettering.

Coach Nos: 7608-7648
Diagram: 2552
Built: 6/49-10/49
Withdrawn: 4/64-12/67
Seating: 7× 1st with 6 seats

No 7648 was the last Bulleid coach to be constructed.

Open Saloon Third — Drawing No 14

These coaches were never allocated to sets but were always kept for 'loose workings' and used for specials, reliefs, or for Ocean Liner Boat trains from Waterloo to Southampton Docks. Some of these coaches were sent to the Eastern and Scottish Regions in 1965.

Coach Nos: 1461-1506
Diagram: 2017
Built: 8/47-1/51
Withdrawn: 1/65-11/68

No 1464 has been preserved.
No 1481 has been preserved.
No 1469 is owned by the Vintage Carriage Trust and is on the Keighley & Worth Valley Railway.
No 1482 is on the Bluebell Railway.

Corridor Compartment Composite — Drawing No 15

In 1946 Eastleigh turned out 18 compartment corridor composites on a short underframe having a length of 59ft over end panels. The four coaches as drawn were the logical development of the earlier ones but extended to the now standard length of 64ft 6in and having one extra third class compartment. When their original sets were disbanded they were downgraded to second class only, but structurally unaltered so it was possible to travel in first class luxury on a second class fare! At the same time the coaches were renumbered S1727-1730.

Coach Nos: 5727-5730
Diagram: 2317
Built: 6/46-7/46
Withdrawn: 9/66-6/67
Seating: 4× 1st with 6 seats
4× 3rd with 8 seats
Notes: In set Nos 981-984

Corridor Compartment Brake Third — Drawing No 16

Developed from the earlier 'short' coaches on the 57ft 11in underframes which were built in 1939/40, these coaches were the earliest recipients of the standard length underframe, which enabled an extra compartment to be fitted.

Coach Nos: 2877-2884
Diagram: 2122
Built: 6/46-7/46
Withdrawn: 12/63-9/67
Seating: 5× 3rd with 8 seats
Notes: In set Nos 981-984

Corridor Brake Third — 59ft — Drawing No 17

The origins of these coaches is mentioned in the Introduction and they became known as 'shorties' after the normal Bulleid coaches had been constructed. They can also be recognised by the length of the guard/luggage compartment which extended over one third of the length of the vehicle plus the fact that two periscopes are fitted in the roof.

Coach Nos: 2841-2876
Diagram: 2121
Built: 11/45-2/46
Withdrawn: 12/63-11/67
Seating: 5 compartments of 8 seats
Notes: Allocated to sets Nos 963-980

No 2850 is preserved on the Mid-Hants Railway

Corridor Composite — 59ft — Drawing No 18

Production following immediately on the above coaches they used the same short underframes. The layout and dimensions between partitions, and some of the fittings, particularly in the lavatories (one each end on these coaches) were virtually the same as the Maunsell composites. There is also a similarity with the Trailer First Corridor coaches of the Hastings demus (Class 201 or 6S) produced 11 years later.

Coach Nos: 5709-5726
Diagram: 2316
Built: 2/46-4/46
Withdrawn: 12/63-12/67
Seating: 4× 1st with 6 seats
3× 3rd with 8 seats

Corridor first coach No 7632. This shows the corridor side.
Ian Allan Library

BRCW-built Bulleid coaches

In order to meet the urgent requirement for new coaches the Southern Railway had a demand that outstripped the capacity at both their Eastleigh and Lancing Works, plus they also had to contend with the shortage of materials as a result of wartime restrictions. Therefore in 1946 orders were placed with the Birmingham Railway Carriage & Wagon Co to build 24 three-coach sets. Delivery was effected between December 1947 and May 1949 at a cost of approx £19,000 per set.

To the uninitiated these three-coach sets looked similar to the normal early Bulleid designed stock built at Eastleigh. However, there were differences, the chief one being the box shaped ventilators with louvred panels projecting from two sides, which were mounted on the roof. The window frames were slightly proud of the coach side and the main windows were 3in shorter and 5in less in depth than the standard Bulleid window while the sliding ventilators were only $10\frac{1}{4}$in deep and were not fitted on the corridor side or in the toilet compartments. The body panels were smaller and had a lapped joint before being screwed to the wooden framing. There was also some detail changes in the ends as shown in the drawings, but these were modified by BR in 1952 when they removed the stepboards above the gangway connections and the upper rainstrip.

Semi-open Brake Third — Drawing No 19

These coaches had a 'one-sided' compartment or 'coupe' nearest the guard's section and then an eight seat compartment with one open saloon seating 32 with a toilet nearest the vestibule, opposite which was a wooden rack for luggage. Interior decor was reminiscent of the Maunsell era with the sides covered in rexine to waist level and then veneer to the ceiling.

Coach Nos: 4209-4228
Diagram: 2124
Built: 12/47-7/48
Withdrawn: 6/58-7/68
Notes: In set Nos 795-804

No 4209 written off in accident.
No 4211 preserved on Mid-Hants Railway.

Corridor Composites — Drawing No 20

Like the coaches described above the corridor windows had no ventilators fitted. These coaches had 4/1st class with 6 seats and 3/3rd with 8 seats. Coaches Nos 5781/2 were fitted with electric heating in the autumn of 1959 for use in the Night Ferry train Victoria-Newhaven.

Coach Nos:	5775-5798	5812-5822
Diagram:	2320	2320
Built:	1/47-5/49	1/47-5/49
Withdrawn	4/64-12/67	4/64-12/67
Notes:	In set Nos 795-818	In set Nos 819-829

Semi-open Brake Third — Drawing No 21

These were virtually the same as coaches 4209-4228 except that the half compartment (or coupe) was replaced with a full compartment the space being made available by reducing the size of the guard's section.

Coach Nos:	4229-4230	4251-4298
Diagram:	2125	2125
Built:	8/48-5/49	8/48-5/49
Withdrawn:	3/56-5/68	3/56-5/68
Notes:	In set No 805	In set Nos 806-829

No 4281 written off in accident.
No 4279 preserved on Bluebell Railway.

▲ A train on the preserved Bluebell Railway the leading coach of which is a BRCW-built semi-open brake third No 4279. This is one of the coaches forming the 'Atlantic Coast' set used on this railway. *Brian Stephenson*

▶ Close up view of brake end of BRCW-built semi-open brake third showing the window frames which were slightly proud of the sides. *G. Pinder*

The Tavern Car Sets

Probably the most controversial railway coach design from the post World War 2 era to the present day was the two-coach Tavern sets as designed by Bulleid and introduced in 1949. One of his first designs for the Southern Railway was the Buffet cars for the 4BUF electric sets on the Victoria-Bognor-Portsmouth line in 1938 and although quite conventional they employed some novel features and it was found that passengers were too comfortable and lingered in the buffet car to the detriment of waiting customers and consequently on sales! Bulleid learnt his lesson and thus the interior of the Tavern Cars were to an ultra modern design and reminiscent of a milk bar! Windows were conspicuous by their absence and there seemed little inclination for passengers to stop in such claustrophobic and cell-like surroundings.

If the actual Tavern Car (Buffet/kitchen car) interior looked like an olde world inn the exterior looked even more incongruous — especially as it was still a railway coach.

Both types of vehicle were on the normal Bulleid underframe and fitted with standard pattern ends, although some modification to the brakegear and underchassis fittings were made.

The sets were not confined to the Southern Region and the original allocation was:

'Atlantic Coast Express' (SR) (Two sets)
'Master Cutler' (ER)
'White Rose'
'Norfolkman'
'Country Continental' (two sets)
'South Yorkshireman' (ER and LMR)

In early 1950 Restaurant car No 7836 was withdrawn for modifications and emerged with orthodox windows and deep ventilators and the seating in the first class reverted to normal with loose chairs, although this reduced the seating from 64 to 54. All the Restaurant vehicles were thus altered between June 1950 and June 1951 and returned paired with a Tavern Car on the Waterloo-West of England services. Soon after this the Tavern Cars began to appear without the timber and brickwork painted on their exteriors reverting to the then standard BR crimson and cream.

Tavern Cars — Buffet Kitchen Car   Drawing No 22

The incongruous appearance of the outside of the vehicle was highlighted by the impression that it was two separate vehicles joined together in the middle and, apart from the then BR livery of crimson and cream, it was further emphasised by one half being adorned with mock tudor wooden beams!

The kitchen half of the coach closely resembled the kitchen side of the Kitchen and Dining Third (Drawing No 6) for the six-coach Bournemouth sets, but there the similarity ended for the other half of the vehicle, which only had two ventilator windows just under the cant rail, was painted to look like an old world pub. The lower half was lined out to represent a brick wall with the upper half having black beams painted on a cream background to complete a mock tudor effect. In the centre of the vehicle a panel was painted with a typical pub sign on a pale blue background. Even the door was painted to represent wooden planking.

Inside the coach the kitchen compartment was fairly conventional and incorporated a staff compartment (plus toilet) with forced air ventilation similar to the Restaurant cars in the six-coach Bournemouth sets. The Tavern half, which seated 12, was fitted with mock dark oak beams both longitudinally on the sides and across the roof against a ceiling having a whitewashed effect. From the ceiling beams imitation metal lanterns were hung, while the floor was composition tiling to depict the old fashioned red and black tiles. The bar at the kitchen end of the vehicle was faced with light oak veneer and buff coloured plastic laminates. The snack counter was stainless steel and plastic.

Eight of the two-coach sets were built:

No 7892	'At the sign of the White Horse'	coupled to Dining Coach No 7833
No 7893	'At the sign of the Jolly Tar'	coupled to Dining Coach No 7834
No 7894	'At the sign of the Dolphin'	coupled to Dining Coach No 7835
No 7895	'At the sign of the Bull'	coupled to Dining Coach No 7836
No 7896	'At the sign of the Salutation'	coupled to Dining Coach No 7837
No 7897	'At the sign of the Three Plovers'	coupled to Dining Coach No 7838
No 7898	'At the sign of the Green Man'	coupled to Dining Coach No 7839
No 7899	'At the sign of the George & Dragon'*	coupled to Dining Coach No 7840

* Originally to have been called 'At the sign of the Crown'

The vehicles were rebuilt in 1959/60 and were finally withdrawn between 11/66 and 12/67.

The Old English Tavern type of sign which adorned the side of the Buffet Kitchen cars. This was on coach No 7892.
British Rail

Interior of the Tavern Car (Buffet/Kitchen car). Note the imitation beams on the roof and doorway from other sections of the coach. *British Rail*

A superb exact 7mm scale model of a Tavern Car in its original condition built by Derek Lucas. *S. W. Stevens-Stratten*

An interior view of the 7mm scale model by Derek Lucas. Even the saucepans on the stove have tomato sauce in them. *S. W. Stevens-Stratten*

Tavern Car — 1st/3rd Restaurant Car (Tavern Trailer) Drawing No 23

These vehicles were the dining room part of the Tavern Car sets and were noted for having no windows except the small ventilators below the cant rail. Therefore meals were taken in surroundings not unlike a prison cell, and one had to stand-up to look out. Following a deluge of complaints, especially when the sets were in service on the Eastern Region, the vehicles were rebuilt with orthodox windows in 1950/51. The original seating in the first class section was 12 straight backed seats against each side (a total of 24), with a small table in front of them which was fitted with a guard rail on the outside. This left a wide gangway for the serving staff, probably the only redeeming feature of their design. Carpet covered the floor and underneath each table was a rubber footmat. The seats were covered in a brocade material having an old rose and dull turquoise motif. The third class section held 40 seats in a conventional manner with maroon upholstery. Interior wall coverings were buff coloured plastic laminates with light oak framing. Luggage racks were of toughened glass so that passengers could see if they had left anything behind when they departed. Recessed fluorescent lighting was fitted in the ceilings.

Coach Nos: 7833-7840
Diagram: 2665
Built: 4/49-6/49
Rebuilt: 6/50-6/51
Withdrawn: 2/65-8/67

Rebuilt Tavern Car — Composite Dining Saloons Drawing No 24

As stated in the section dealing with the Tavern Cars as originally built, there was severe and voluminous criticism both in the press and by communications sent direct to British Railways and the Railway Executive, regarding the design of these vehicles. Condemnation came from passengers on every route on which they worked and they proved so unpopular with regular passengers that the dining cars were deserted, especially the first class and financial takings dropped to an all-time low.

The first coach to be rebuilt was No 7836 which was returned to Eastleigh early in 1950 to be followed by the other seven during May of that year.

The rebuilding was quite drastic and in essence changed the vehicles back to a conventional looking coach. Normal windows were fitted on both sides and with the deep type ventilators for both first and third class sections, while the first class seating was taken out and the usual pattern of fixed tables with loose chairs was adopted. This reduced the seating capacity in the first class section from 24 to 18. Seating in the third class section remaining the same for 36 persons. However, the classification was changed round and now the first class section was next to the kitchen. The coaches now resembled the Corridor and Dining First as used on the six-car Bournemouth sets, except that they had no central door, merely one at each end.

The vehicles were returned to service, at first slowly, but in time for the peak summer traffic in 1951 and were used mainly on the West of England services paired with a Tavern Car. From 1952 one set was kept for the Waterloo-Weymouth service, then known as the 'Royal Wessex'.

Following their rebuilding the coaches retained the crimson and cream livery until about 1957 when they were repainted green.

In the mid-1960s BR designed some coaches as Open Seconds with kitchen buffet thus the Bulleid coaches became superfluous and the first was withdrawn in February 1965 and by August 1967 all had been scrapped.

Buffet Kitchen Car — Drawing No 25

Apart from the peculiar exterior appearance, these coaches did not quite cause such a violent reaction from the public. However, the first one was repainted in green livery in June 1957 and in 1959 Nos 7892 and 7896 were sent to Eastleigh for rebuilding as conventional kitchen/buffet coaches. This involved fitting normal windows in the sides and a change in the interior arrangements so that the passenger section had two tables with seats on one side of the coach and bar type seating on the other — a total of only 11 seats. The 'inn' sign was abolished at the same time. The interior decor was completely altered and the mock Tudor style discarded to be replaced with normal plastic laminates.

The first coach was withdrawn in November 1966 and the last in December 1967.

The interior of the third class saloon of the Restaurant car. Note the claustrophobic appearance. *Ian Allan Library*

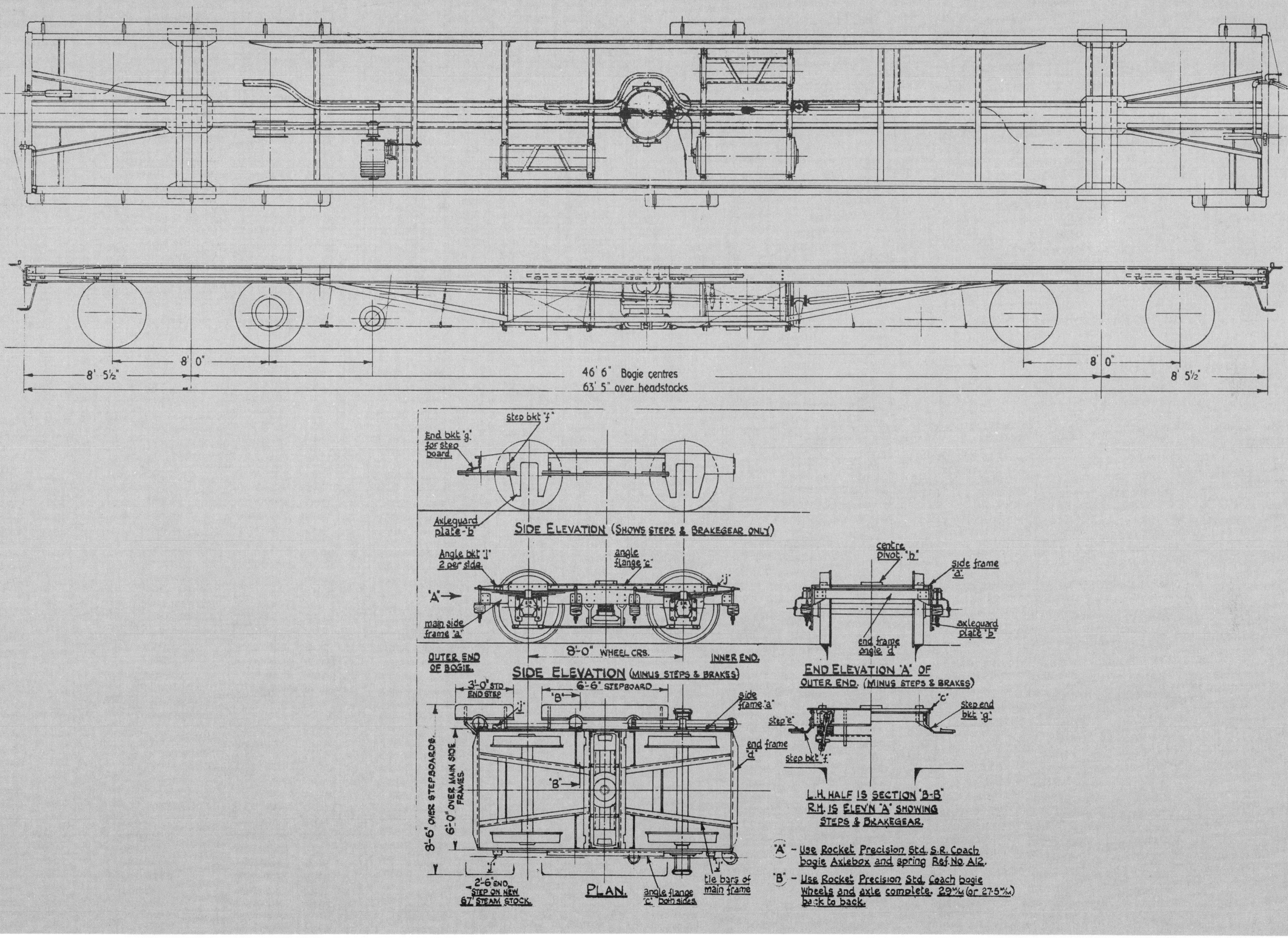
8' 5½"
8' 0"
46' 6" Bogie centres
63' 5" over headstocks
8' 0"
8' 5½"
step bkt 'f'
End bkt 'g' for step board.
Axleguard plate-'b'
SIDE ELEVATION (SHOWS STEPS & BRAKEGEAR ONLY)
Angle bkt 'J' 2 per side.
angle flange 'c'
'j'
'A'
main side frame 'a'
8'-0" WHEEL CRS.
OUTER END OF BOGIE.
INNER END.
SIDE ELEVATION (MINUS STEPS & BRAKES)
centre pivot. 'h'
side frame 'a'
axleguard plate 'b'
end frame angle 'd'
END ELEVATION 'A' OF OUTER END. (MINUS STEPS & BRAKES)
3'-0" STD END STEP
6'-6" STEPBOARD
'B'
'j'
side frame 'a'
end frame 'd'
'B'
8'-6" OVER STEPBOARDS.
6'-0" OVER MAIN SIDE FRAMES.
'j'
'j'
2'-6" END STEP ON NEW 67' STEAM STOCK.
PLAN.
angle flange 'c' both sides.
tie bars of main frame
'c'
step end bkt 'g'
step 'e'
step bkt 'f'
L.H. HALF IS SECTION 'B-B'
R.H. IS ELEV'N 'A' SHOWING STEPS & BRAKEGEAR.
'A' - Use Rocket Precision Std. S.R. Coach bogie Axlebox and spring Ref. No. A12.
'B' - Use Rocket Precision Std. Coach bogie Wheels and axle complete. 29m/m (or 27.5m/m) back to back.

Drawing No 2

End Elevations, all coaches

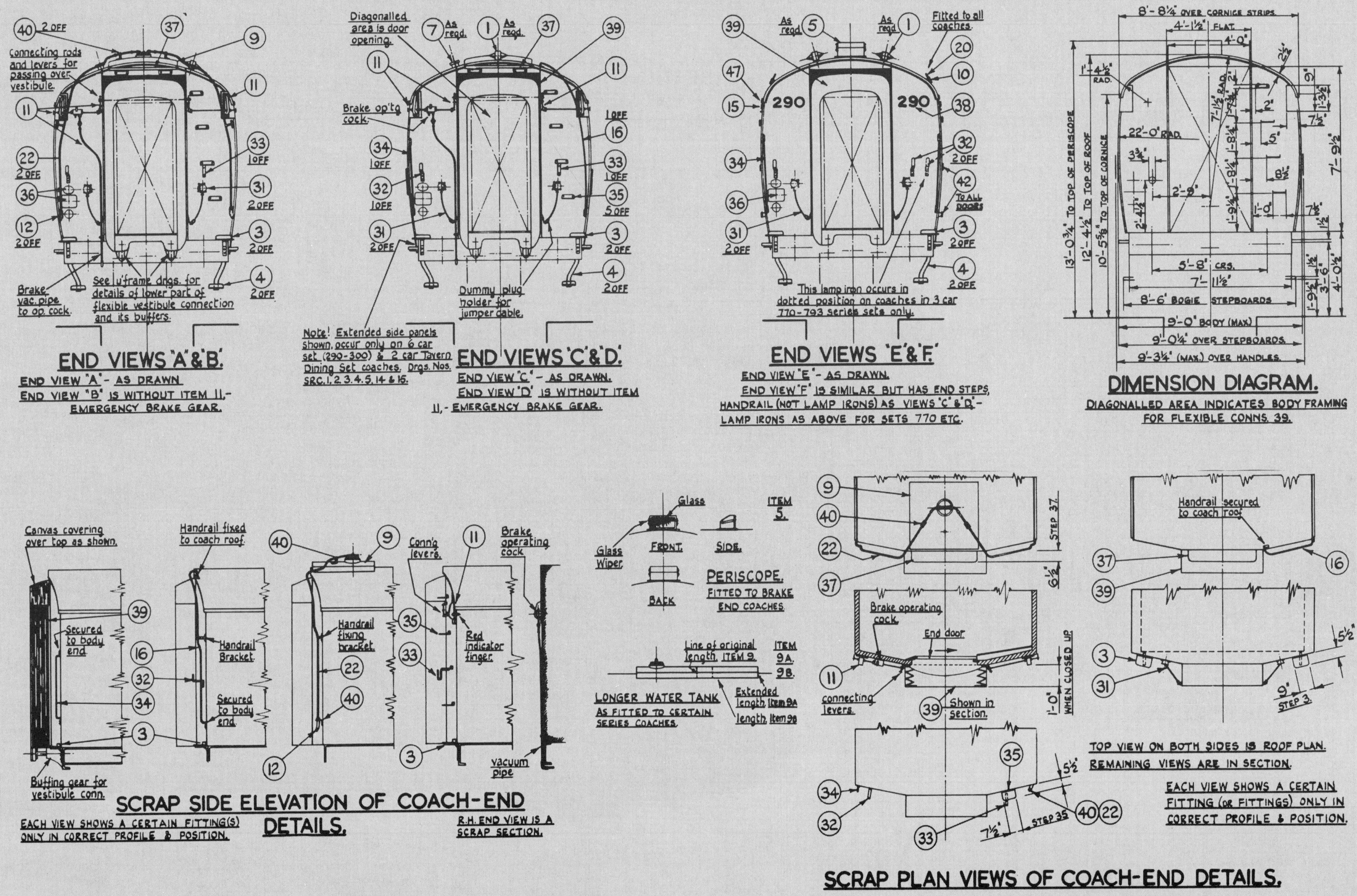

Semi-open Brake Third

Drawing No 3

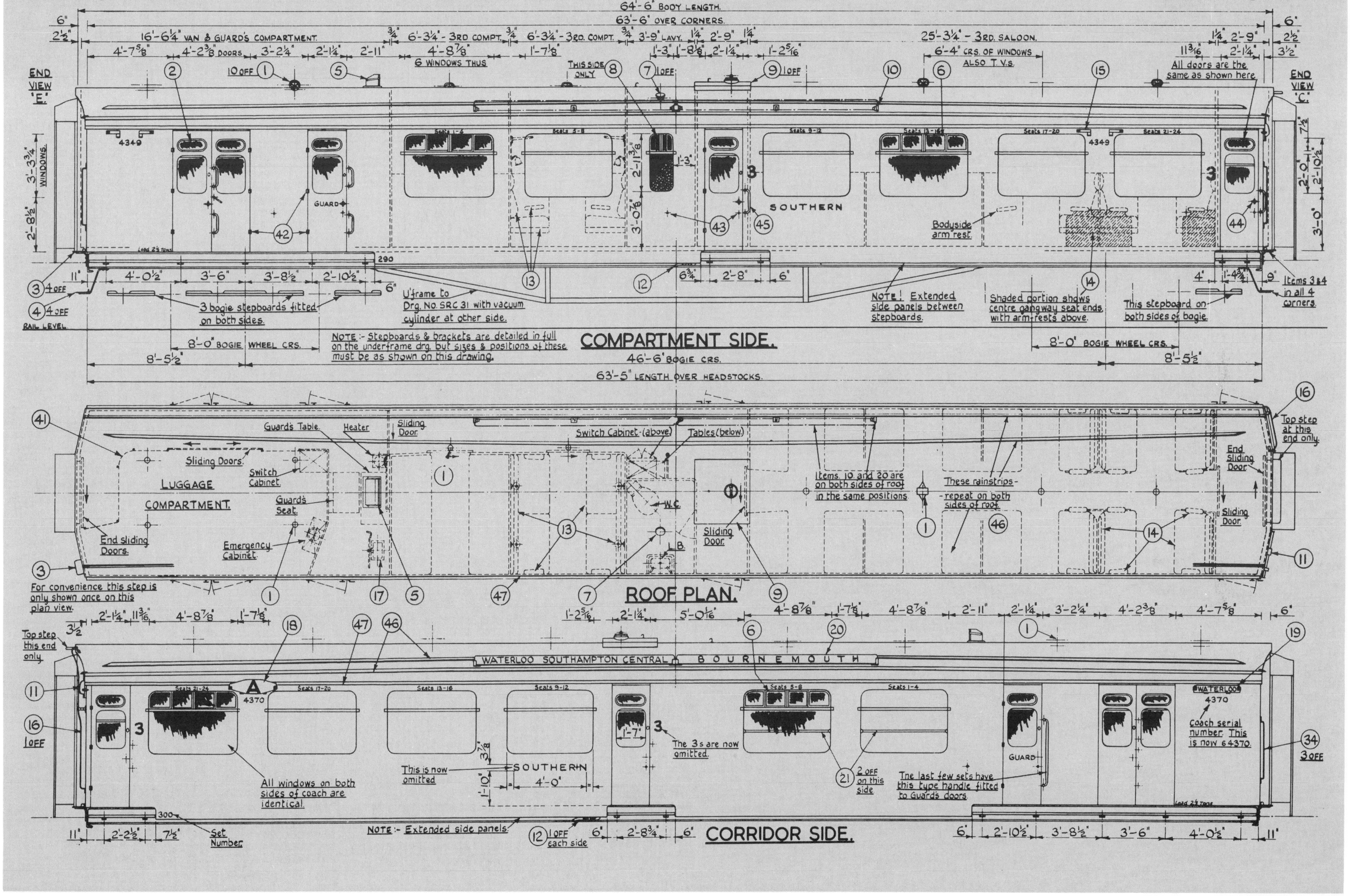

Drawing No 4

Corridor Composite

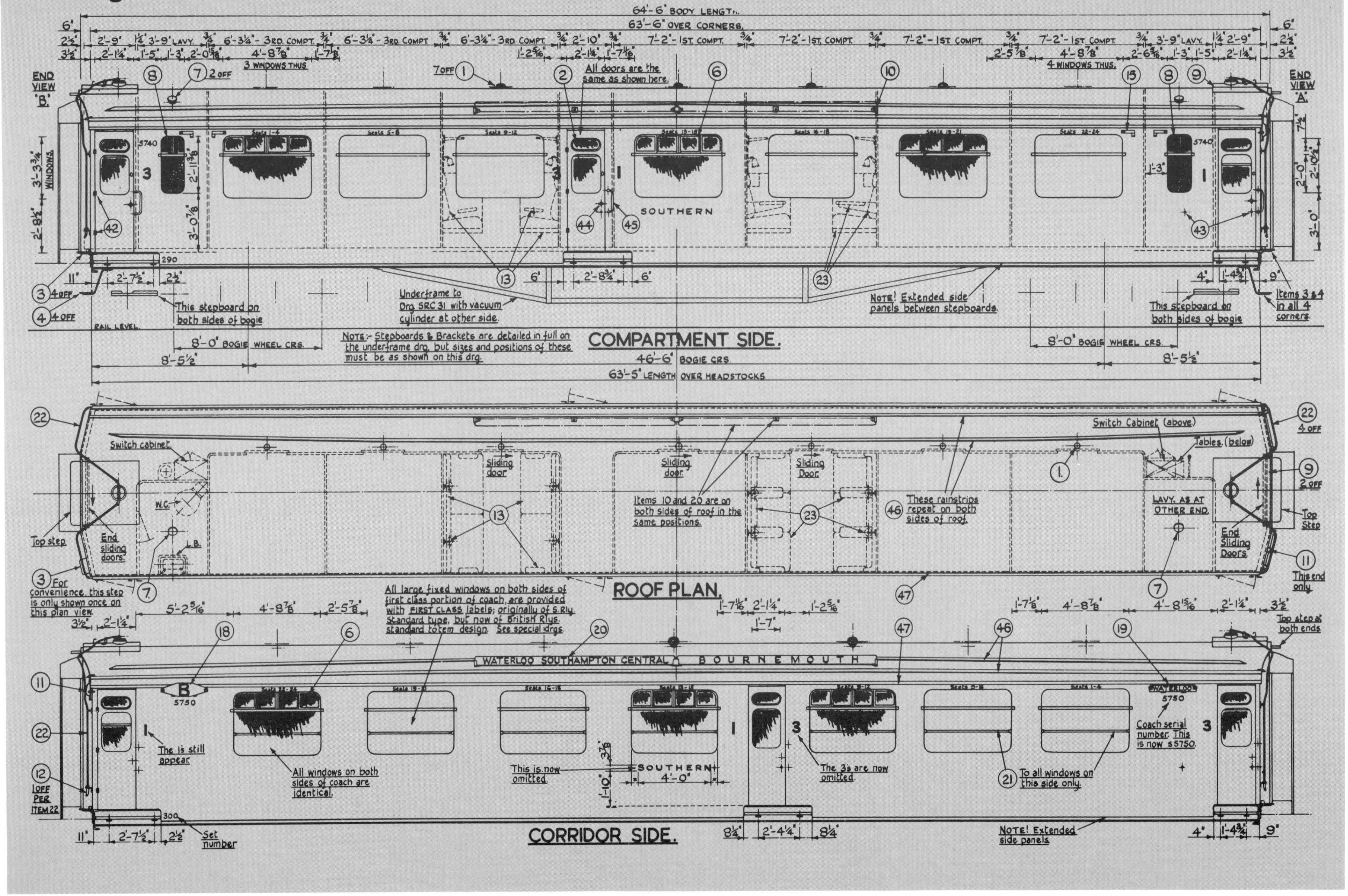

Corridor Dining First

Drawing No 5

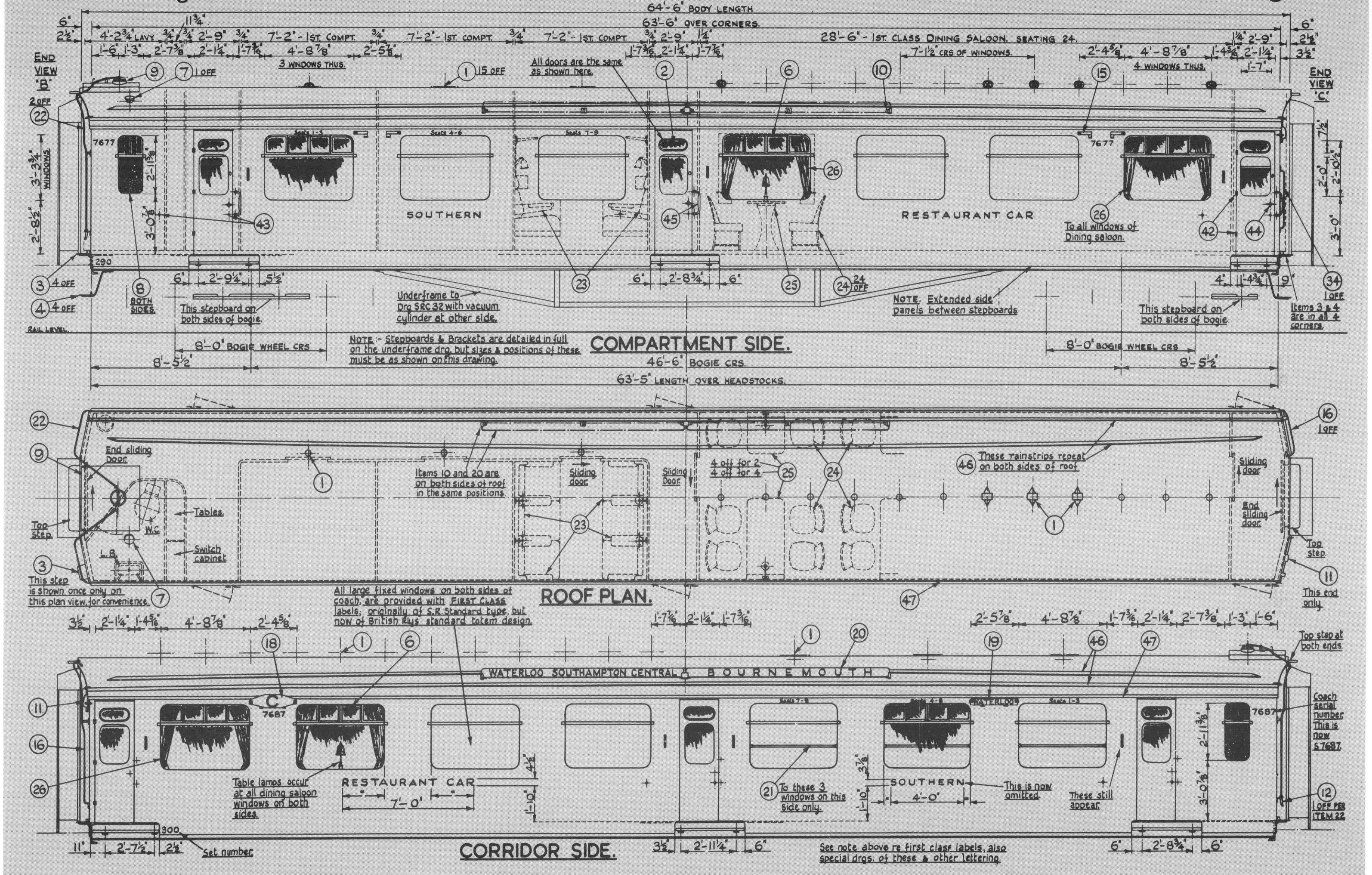

Drawing No 6

Kitchen and Dining Third

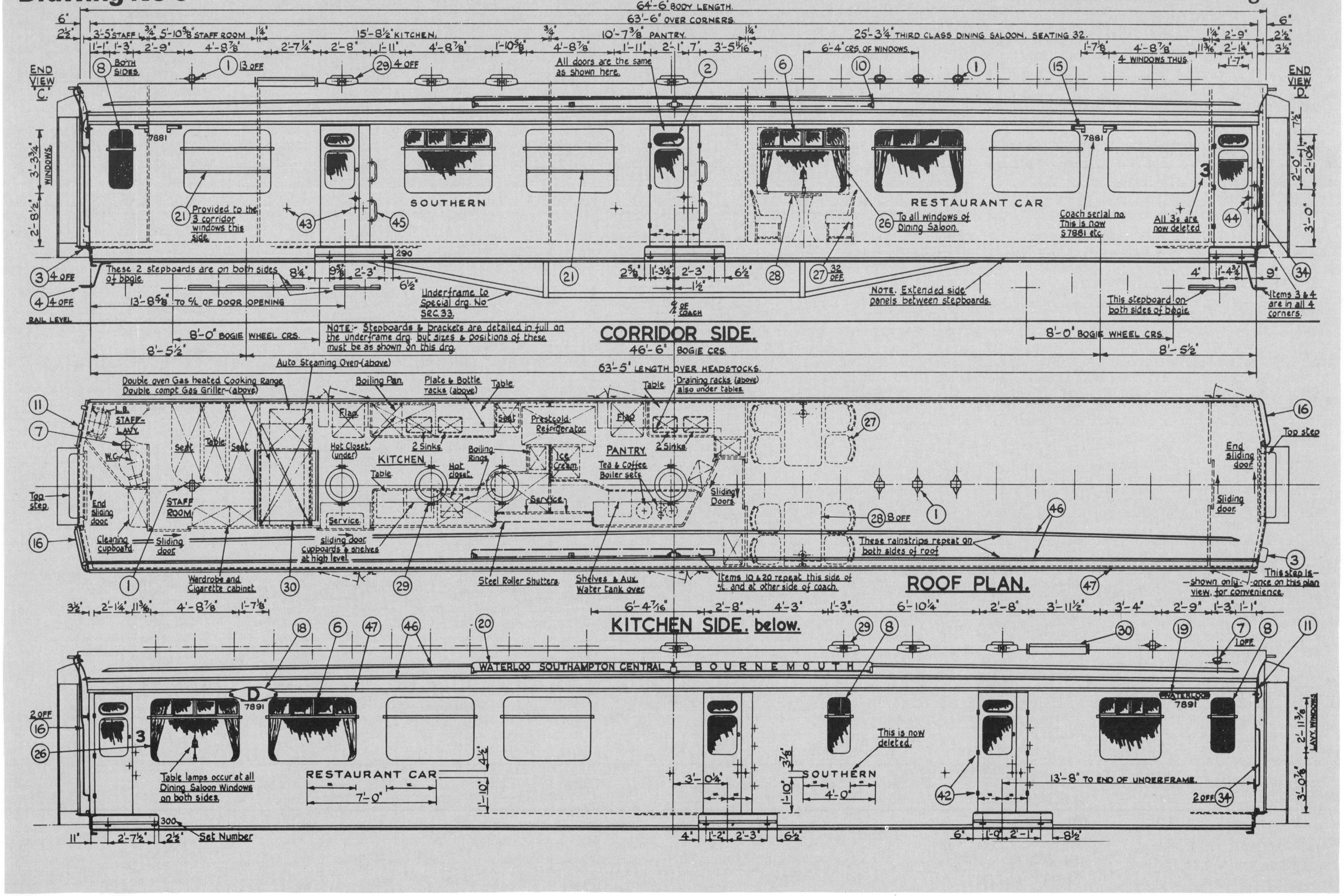

Open Saloon Third

Drawing No 7

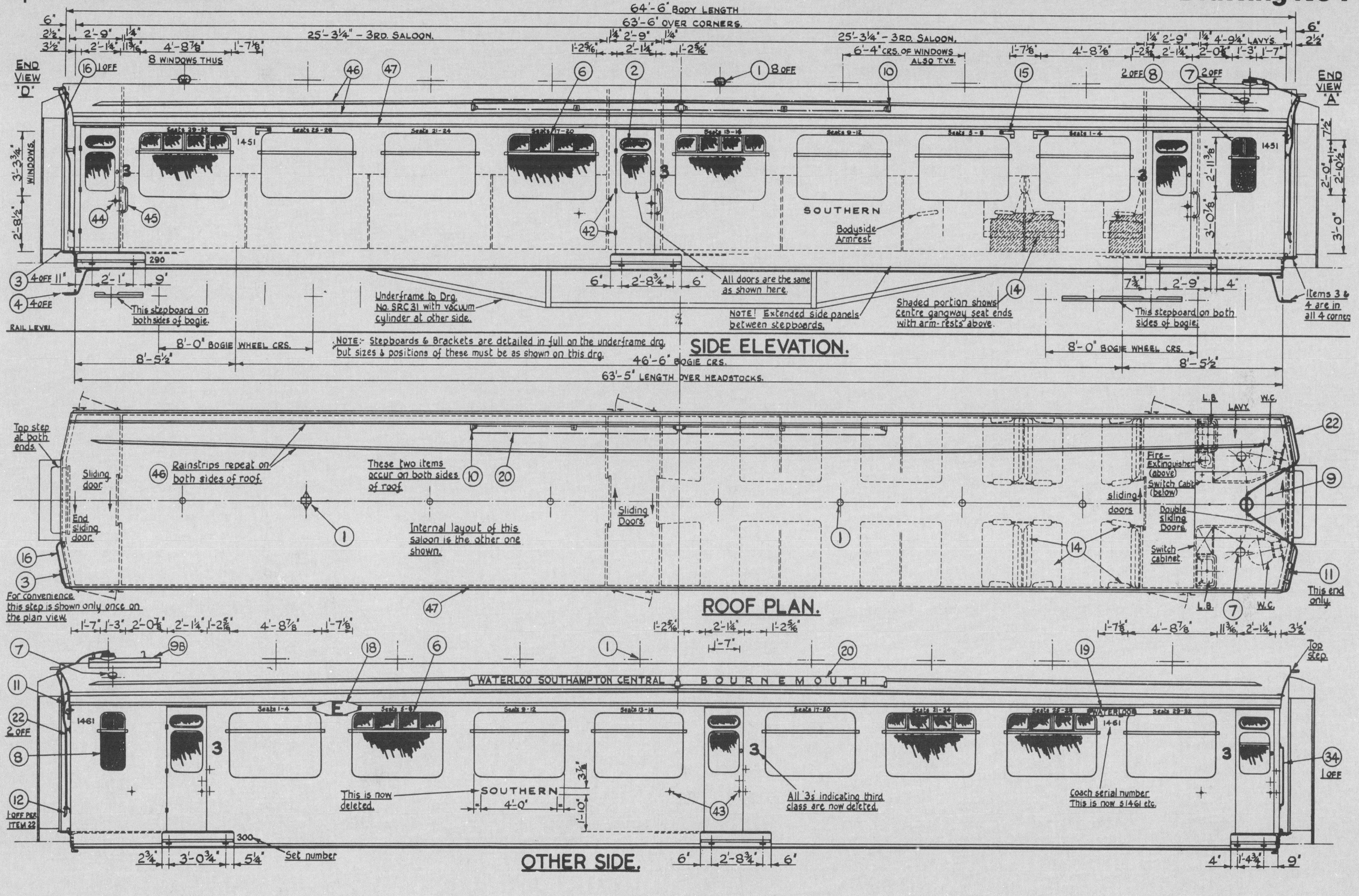

Drawing No 8

Semi-open Brake Third

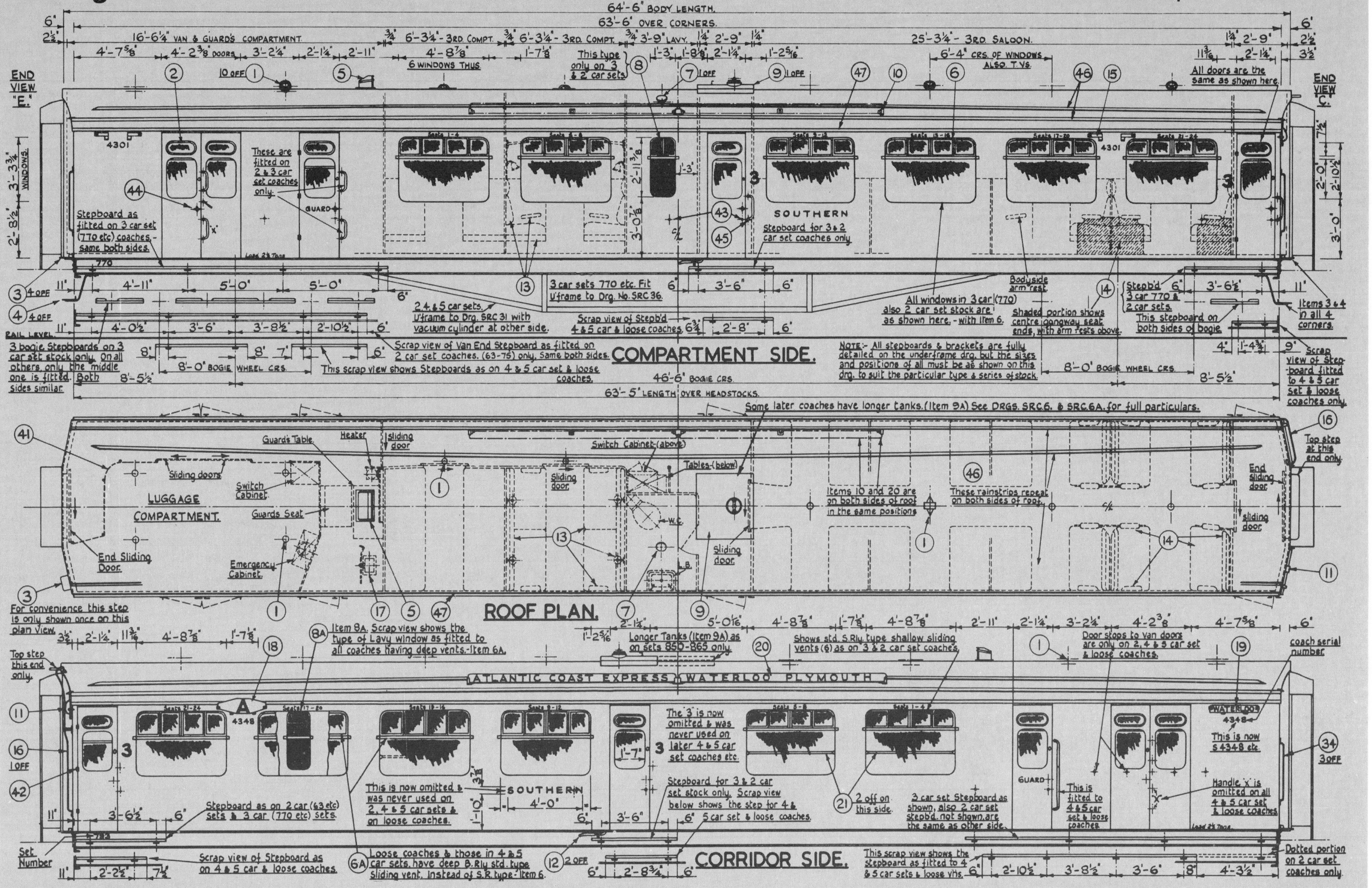

Drawing No 9

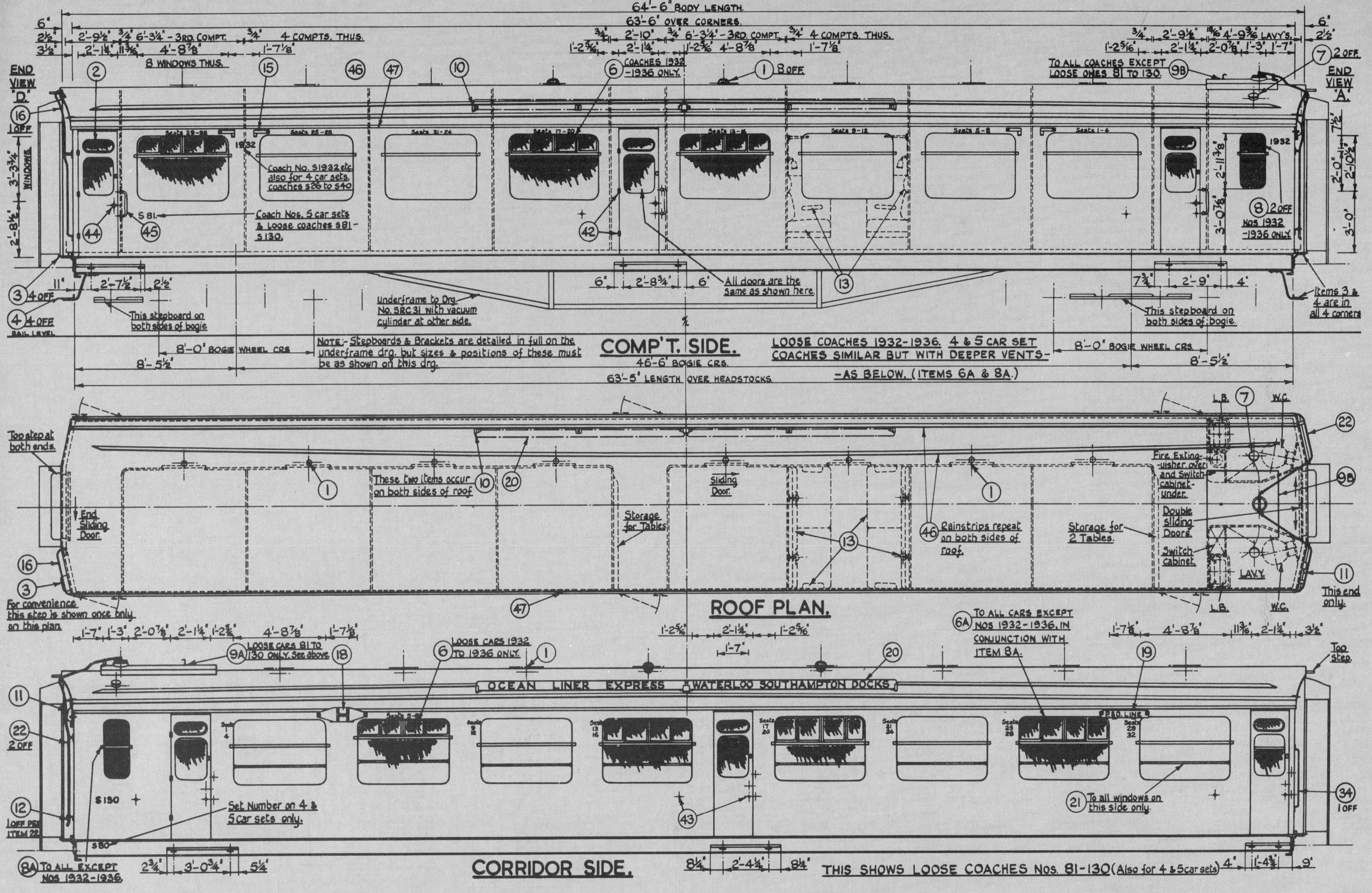

64'-6" BODY LENGTH.
63'-6" OVER CORNERS.
COMP'T. SIDE.
LOOSE COACHES 1932-1936. 4 & 5 CAR SET COACHES SIMILAR BUT WITH DEEPER VENTS- -AS BELOW. (ITEMS 6A & 8A.)
46'-6" BOGIE CRS.
63'-5" LENGTH OVER HEADSTOCKS.
8'-0" BOGIE WHEEL CRS
NOTE:- Stepboards & Brackets are detailed in full on the underframe drg. but sizes & positions of these must be as shown on this drg.
Underframe to Drg. No. SRC31 with vacuum cylinder at other side.
All doors are the same as shown here.
This stepboard on both sides of bogie
Items 3 & 4 are in all 4 corners
Coach No. S1932 etc also for 4 car sets, coaches S26 to S40
Coach Nos. 5 car sets & Loose coaches S81-S130.
COACHES 1932-1936 ONLY.
TO ALL COACHES EXCEPT LOOSE ONES 81 TO 130.
8 WINDOWS THUS.
4 COMPTS. THUS.
END VIEW "D"
END VIEW "A"
ROOF PLAN.
Top step at both ends.
End Sliding Door.
These two items occur on both sides of roof
Sliding Door.
Storage for Tables
Rainstrips repeat on both sides of roof.
Storage for 2 Tables.
Fire Extinguisher over and Switch cabinet under.
Double Sliding Doors.
Switch cabinet.
LAVY.
L.B.
W.C.
This end only.
For convenience this step is shown once only on this plan
CORRIDOR SIDE.
OCEAN LINER EXPRESS WATERLOO SOUTHAMPTON DOCKS
LOOSE CARS 81 TO 130 ONLY. See above.
LOOSE CARS 1932 TO 1936 ONLY.
TO ALL CARS EXCEPT NOS 1932-1936, IN CONJUNCTION WITH ITEM 8A.
Top step.
To all windows on this side only.
Set Number on 4 & 5 car sets only.
TO ALL EXCEPT NOS 1932-1936.
THIS SHOWS LOOSE COACHES NOS. 81-130 (Also for 4 & 5 car sets)

Drawing No 10

Corridor Composite

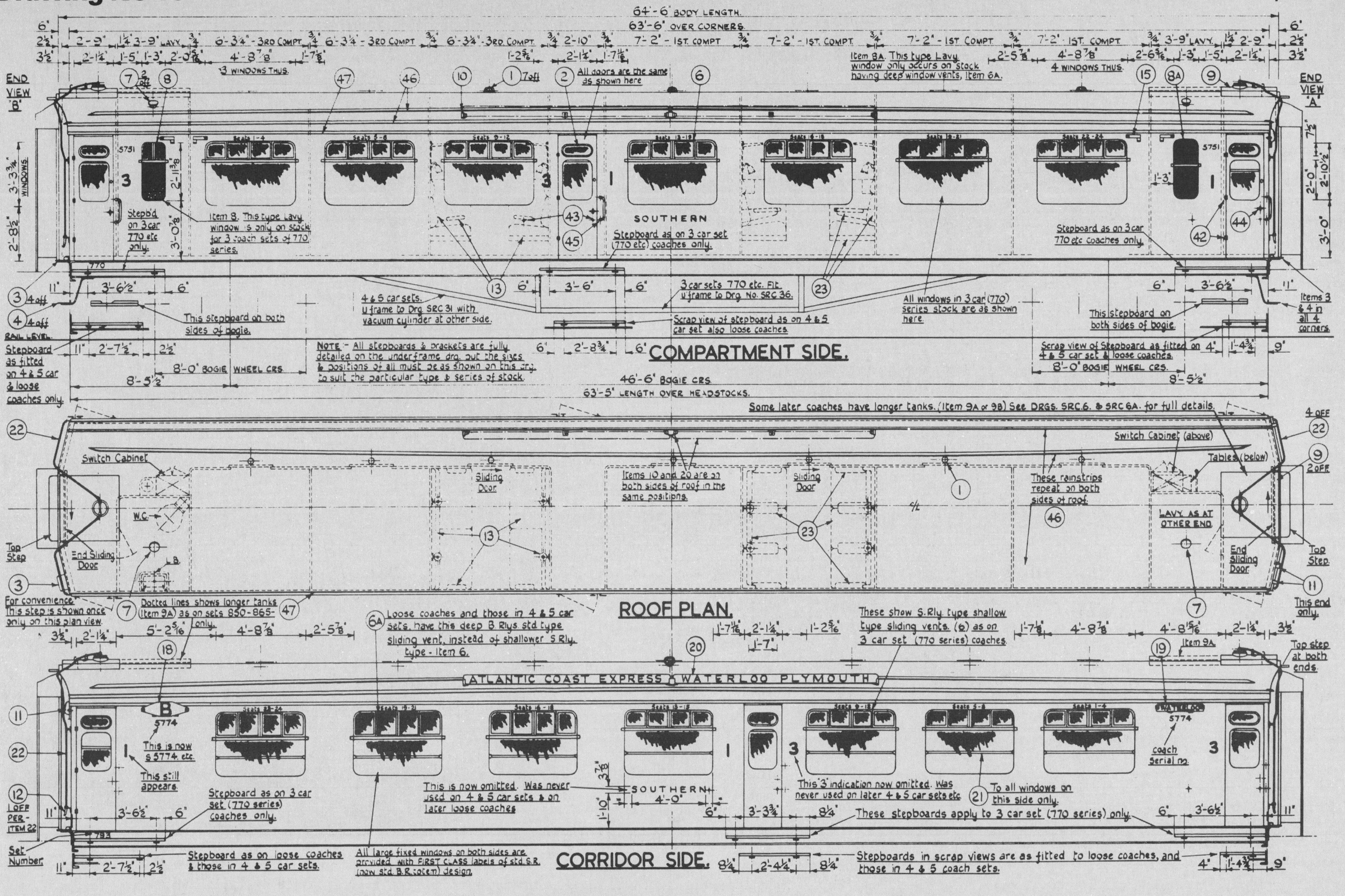

Drawing No 11

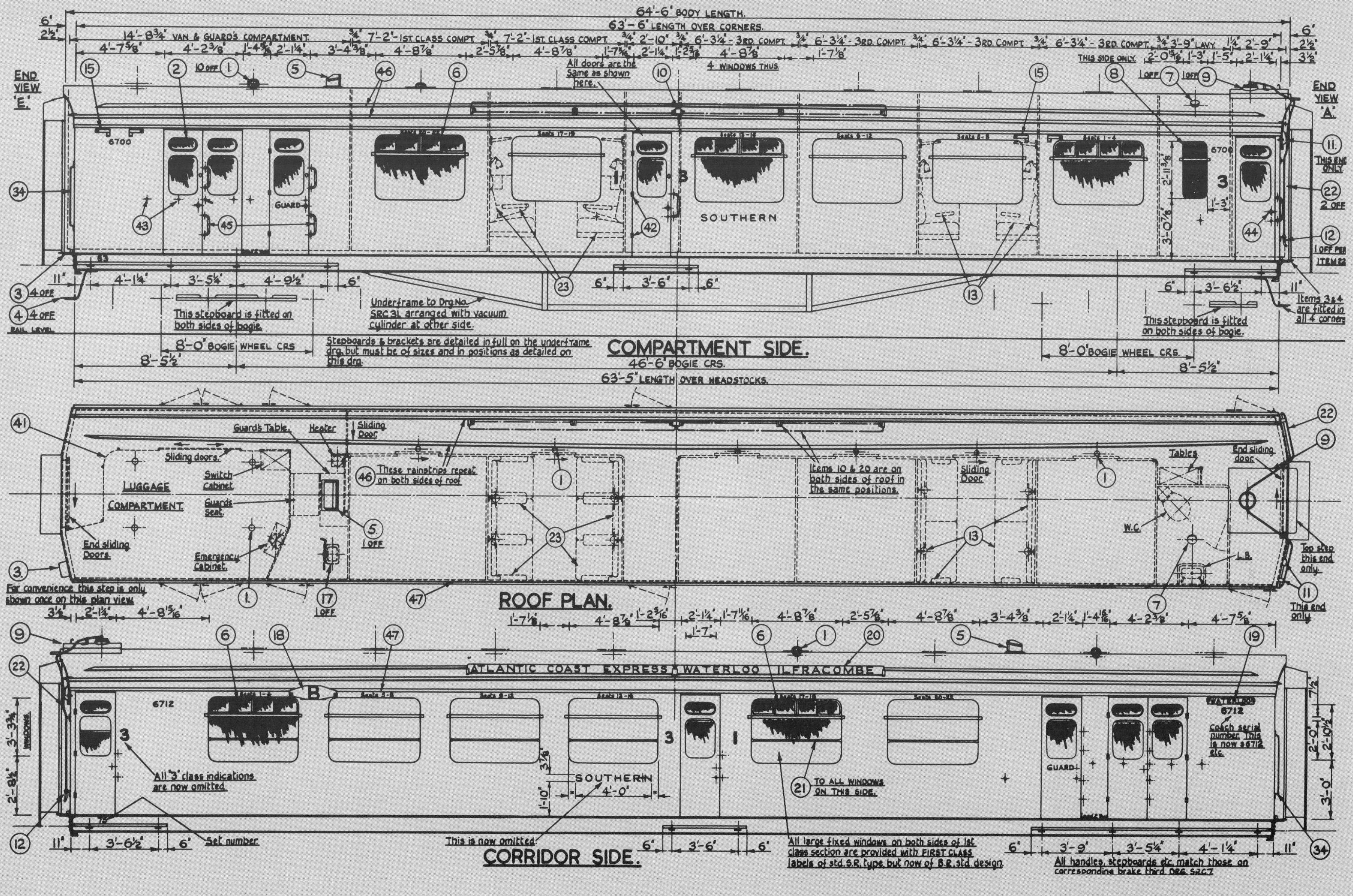

Drawing No 12

Brake Composite

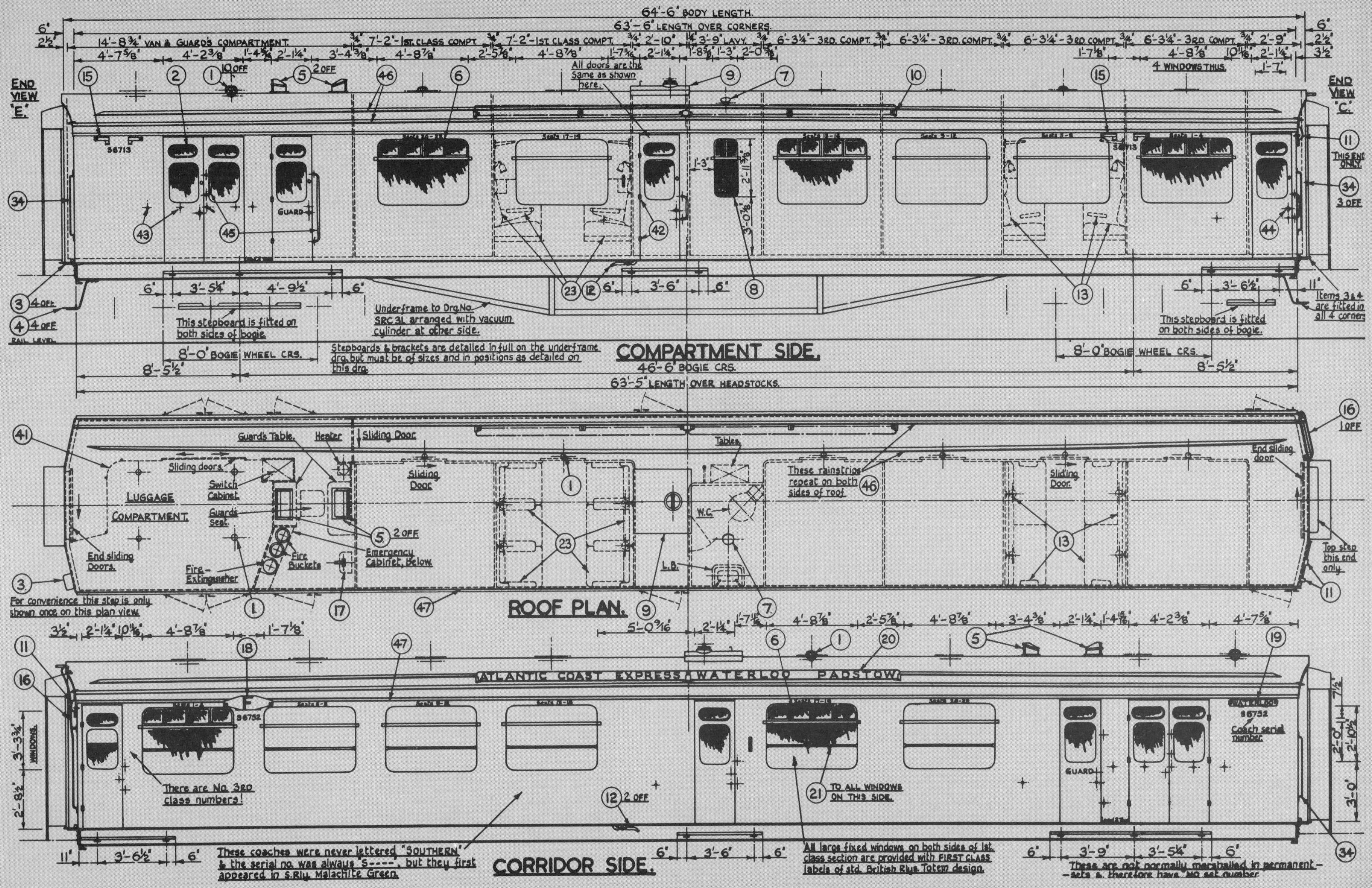

Corridor First

Drawing No 13

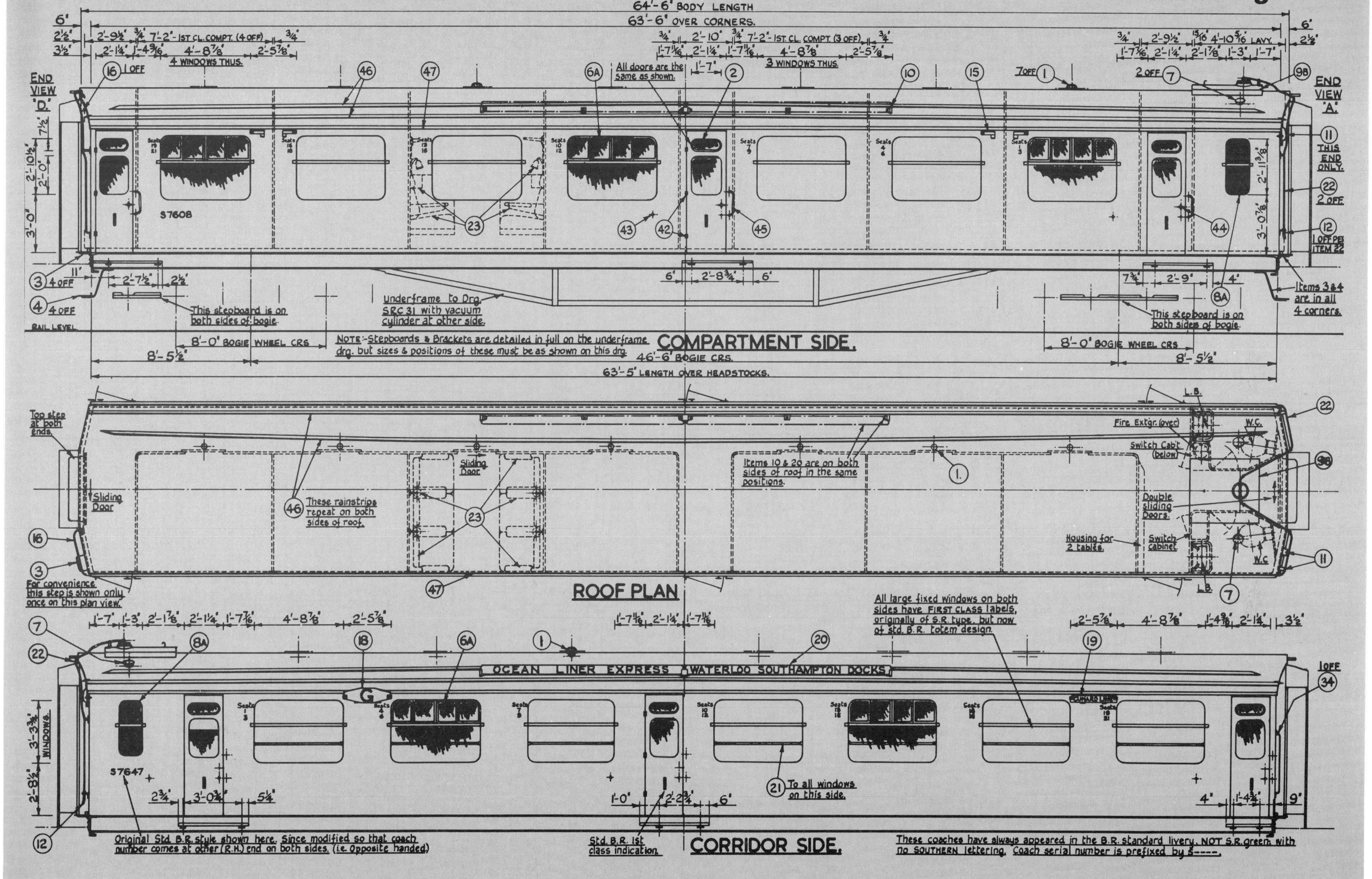

Drawing No 14

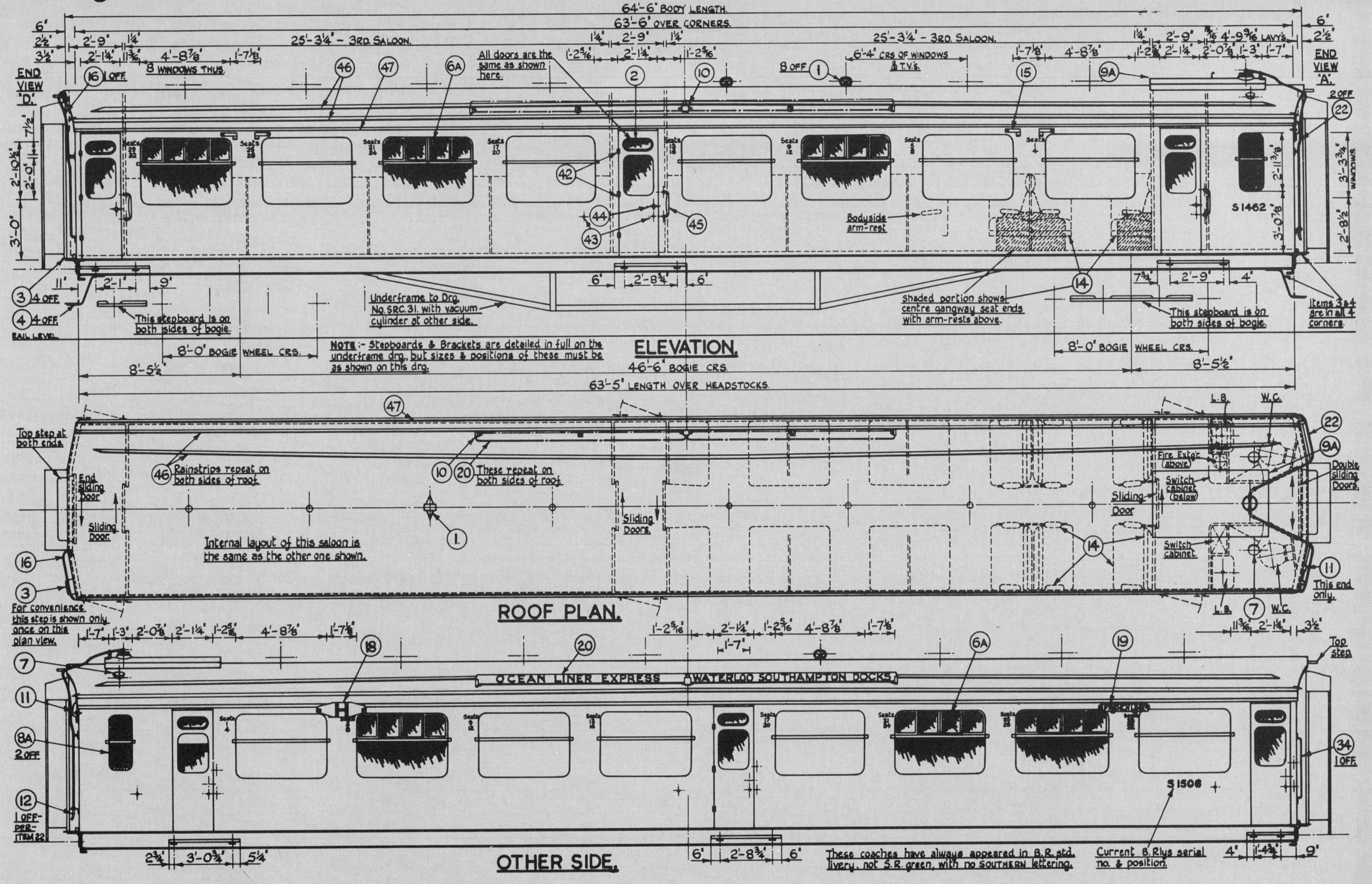

Drawing No 15

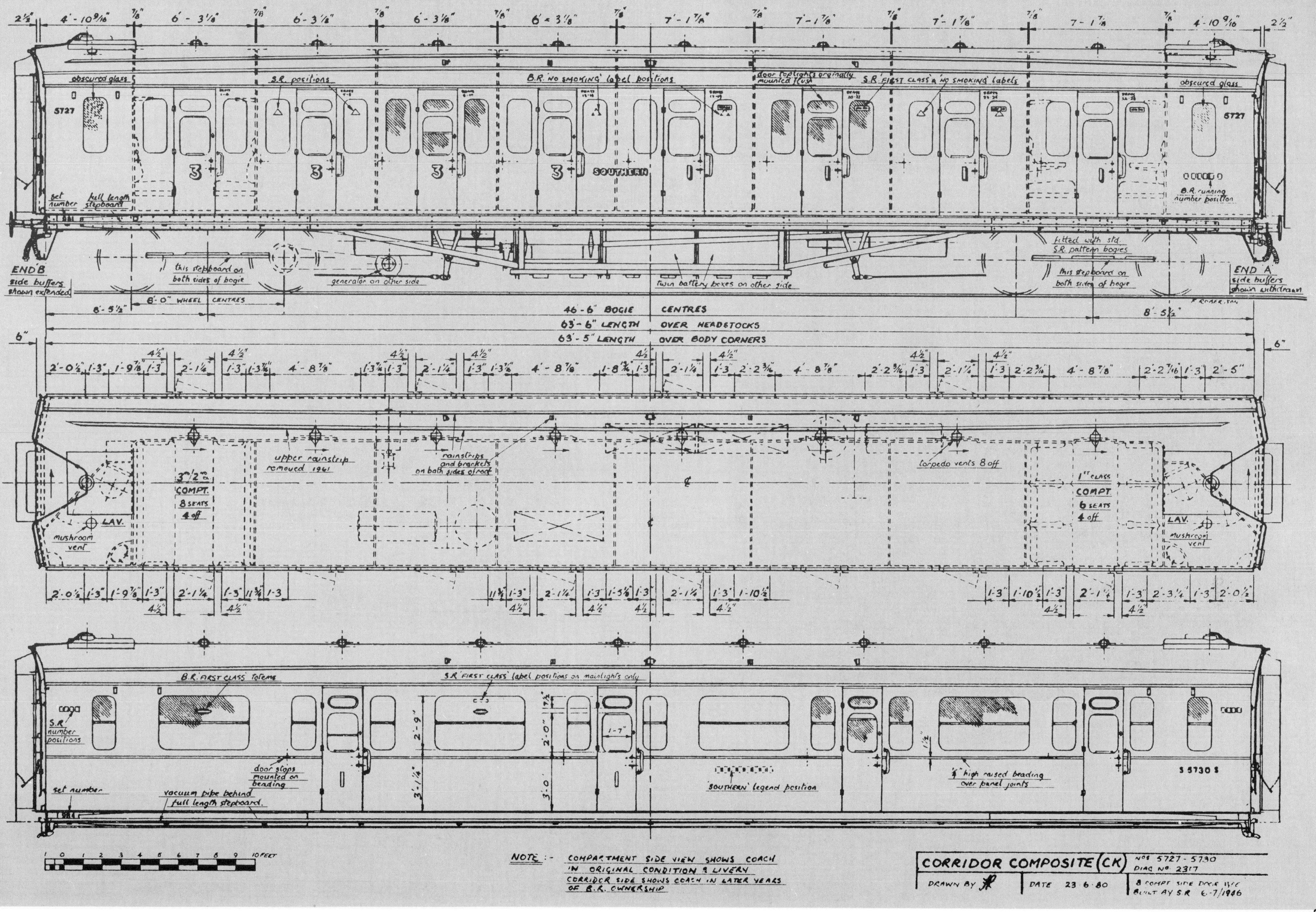

Drawing No 16

Corridor Compartment Brake Third

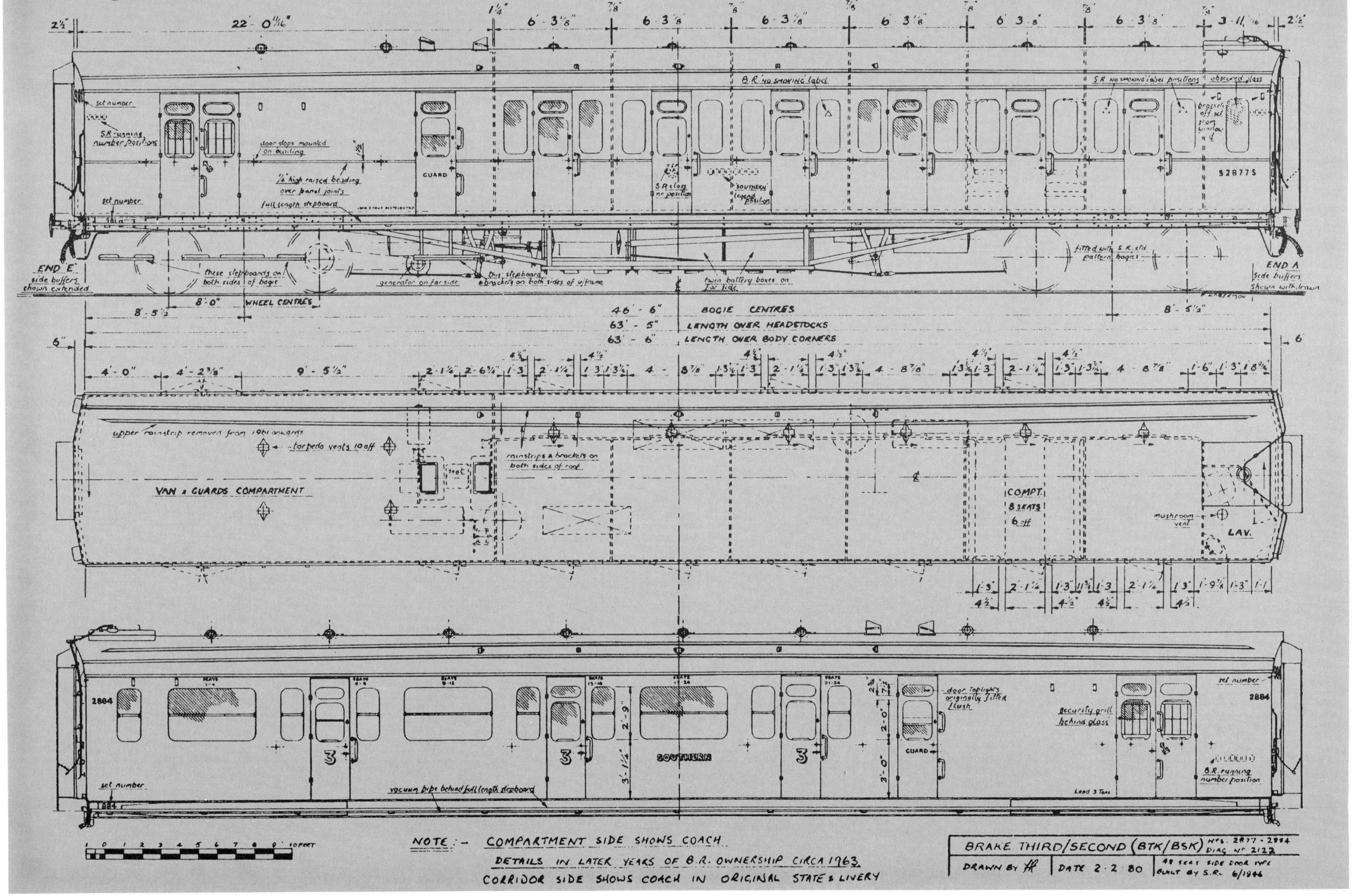

Corridor Brake Third — 59ft

Drawing No 17

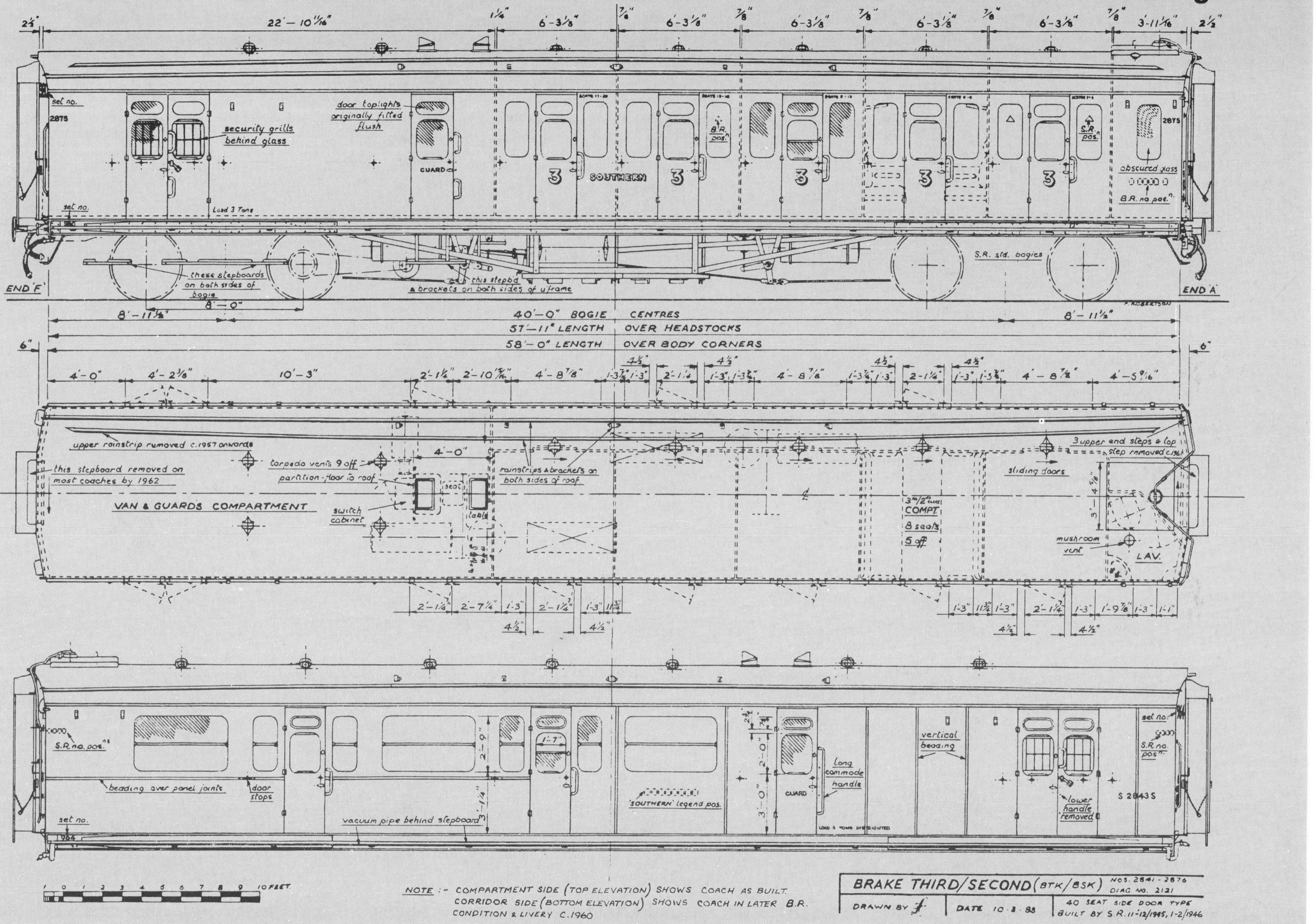

Drawing No 18

Corridor Composite — 59ft

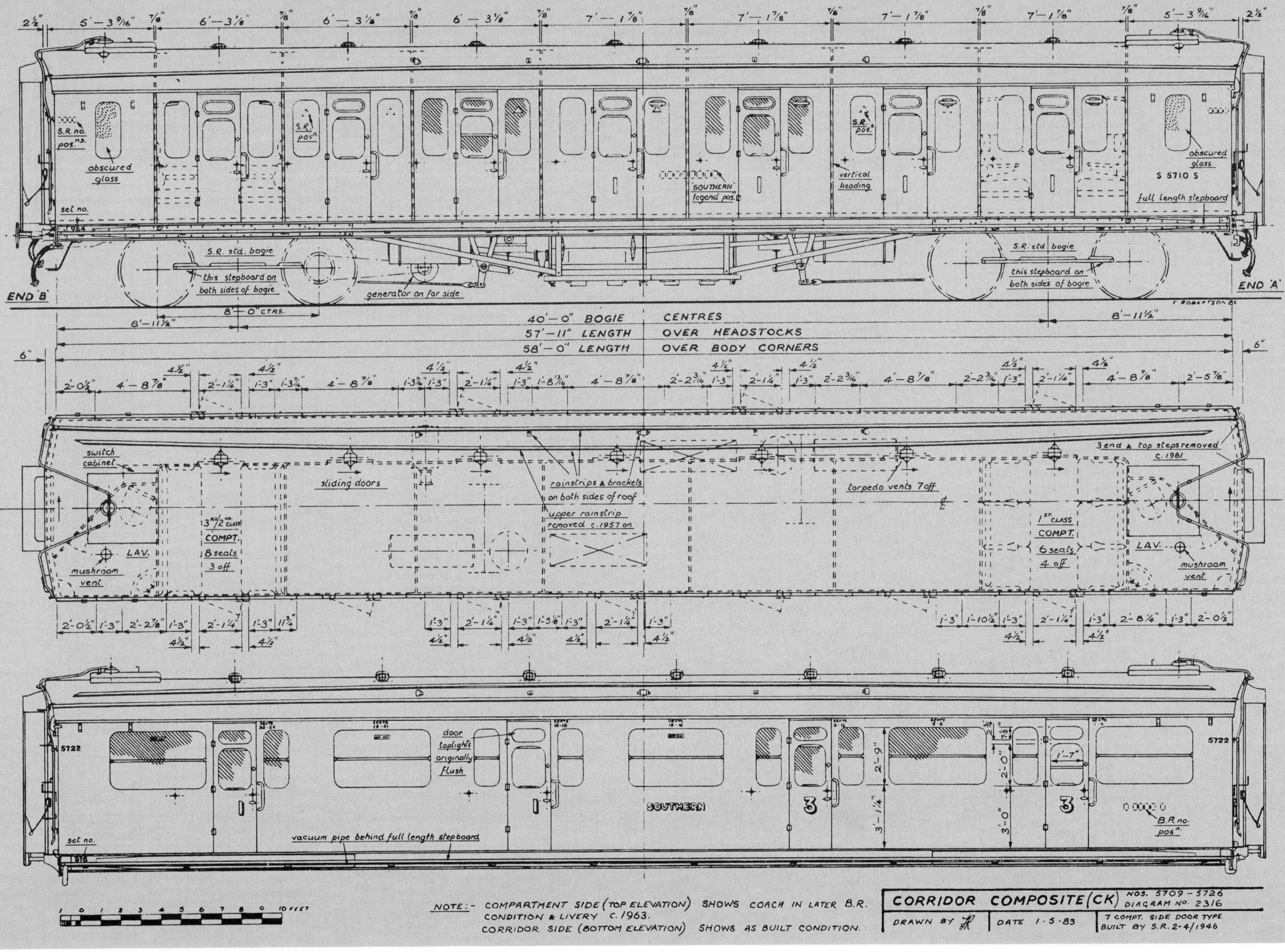

Drawing No 19

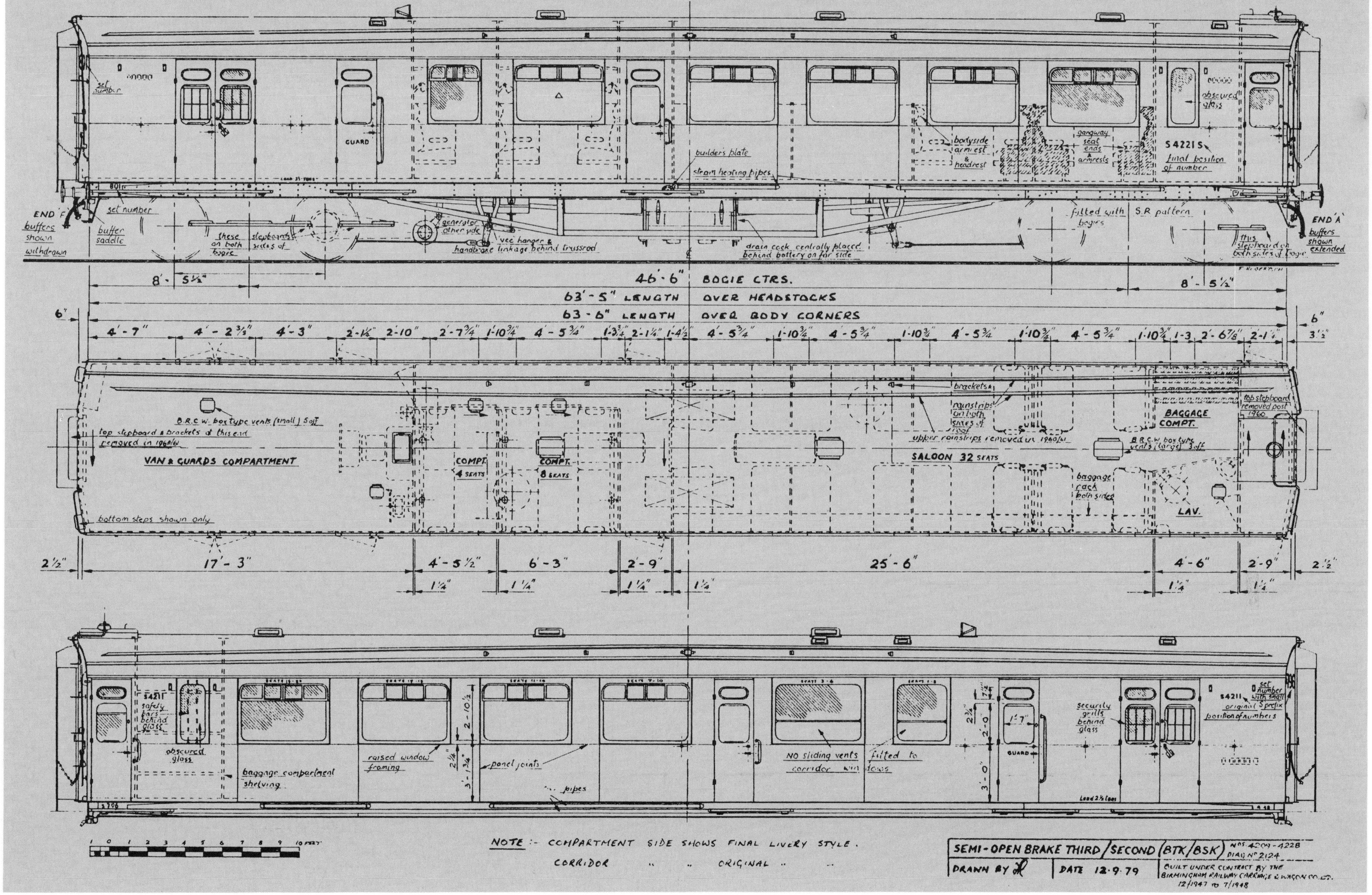

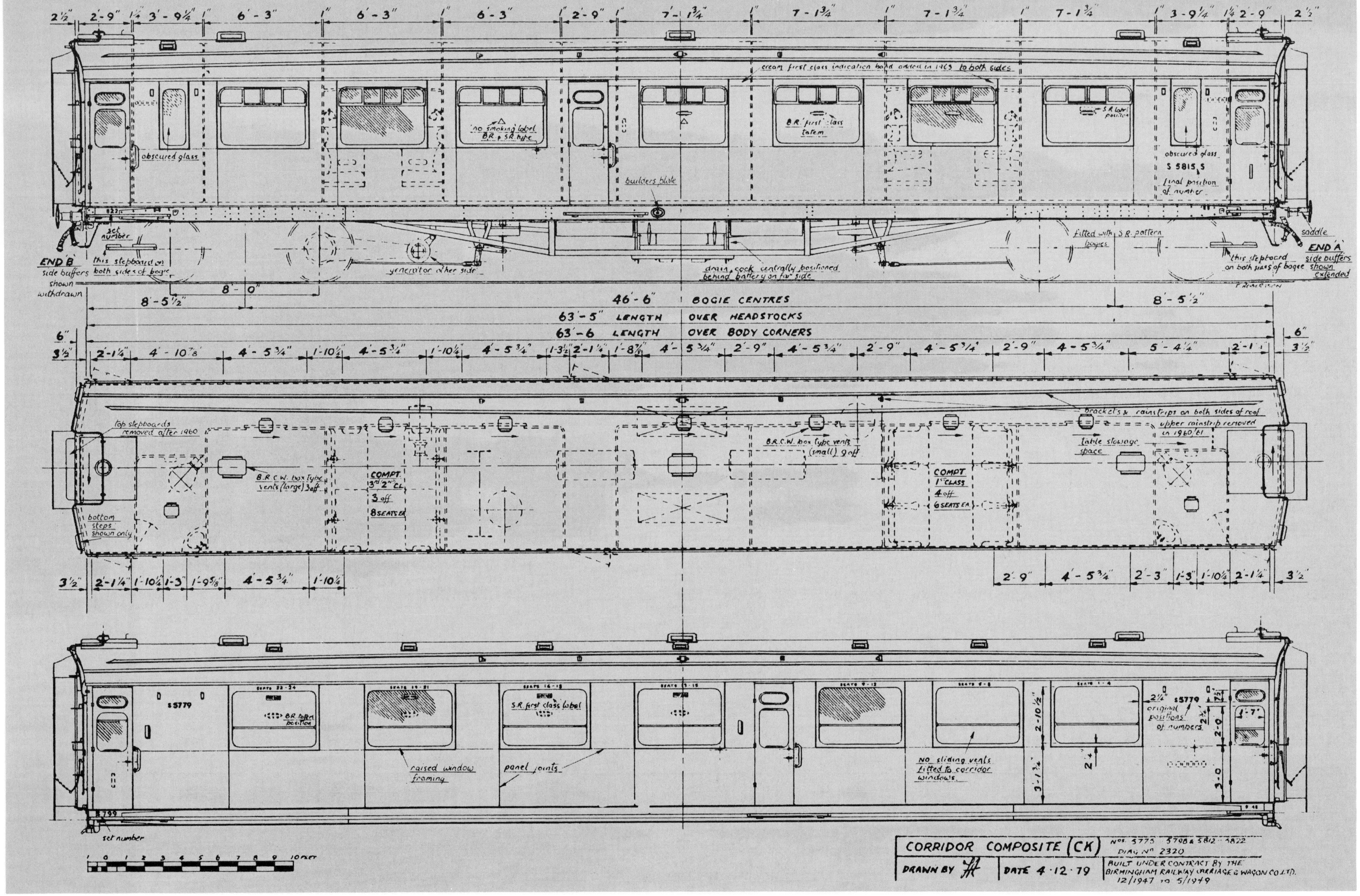
cream first class indication band added in 1963 to both sides
obscured glass
'no smoking' label BR & SR type
builders plate
B.R. 'first' class totem
obscured glass
S 5815 S
final position of number
set number
END 'B'
side buffers shown withdrawn
this stepboard on both sides of bogie
yenerator other side
drain cock centrally positioned behind battery on far side
fitted with S.R. pattern bogies
saddle
END 'A'
side buffers shown extended
this stepboard on both sides of bogie
BOGIE CENTRES
LENGTH OVER HEADSTOCKS
LENGTH OVER BODY CORNERS
top stepboards removed after 1960
B.R.C.W. box type vents (large) 3 off
bottom steps shown only
COMPT 3rd 2nd CL 3 off 8 SEATS EA
B.R.C.W. box type vents (small) 9 off
brackets & rainstrips on both sides of roof
upper rainstrip removed in 1960/61
table stowage space
COMPT 1st CLASS 4 off 6 SEATS EA
S 5779
B.R. totem position
S.R. first class label
raised window framing
panel joints
No sliding vents fitted to corridor windows
original positions of numbers
set number
CORRIDOR COMPOSITE (CK)
Nos 5775 5798 & 5812 – 5822
DIAG No 2320
DRAWN BY
DATE 4·12·79
BUILT UNDER CONTRACT BY THE BIRMINGHAM RAILWAY CARRIAGE & WAGON CO LTD.
12/1947 to 5/1949

Semi-open Brake Third

Drawing No 21

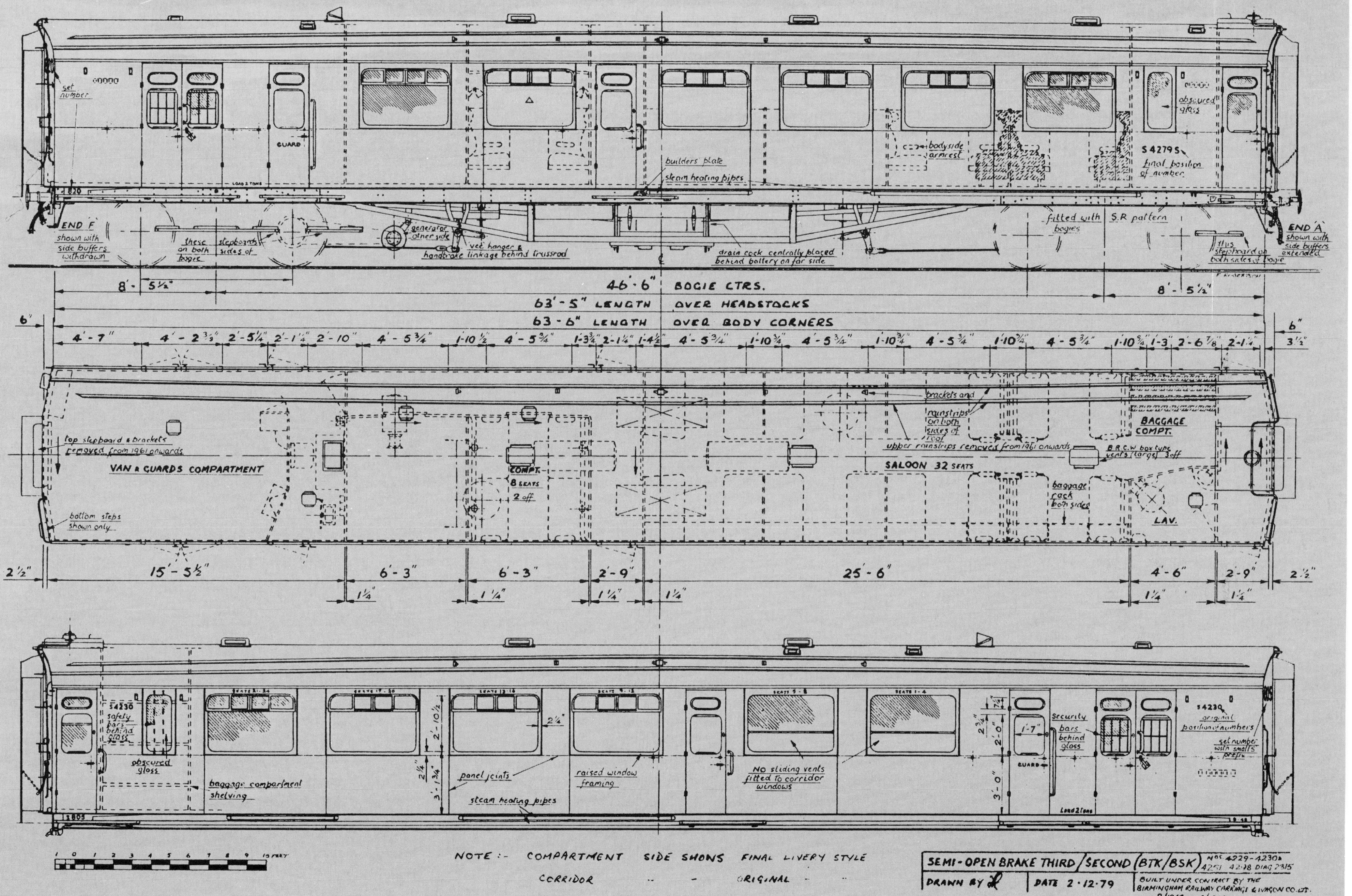

Drawing No 22

Tavern Car — Buffet Kitchen Car

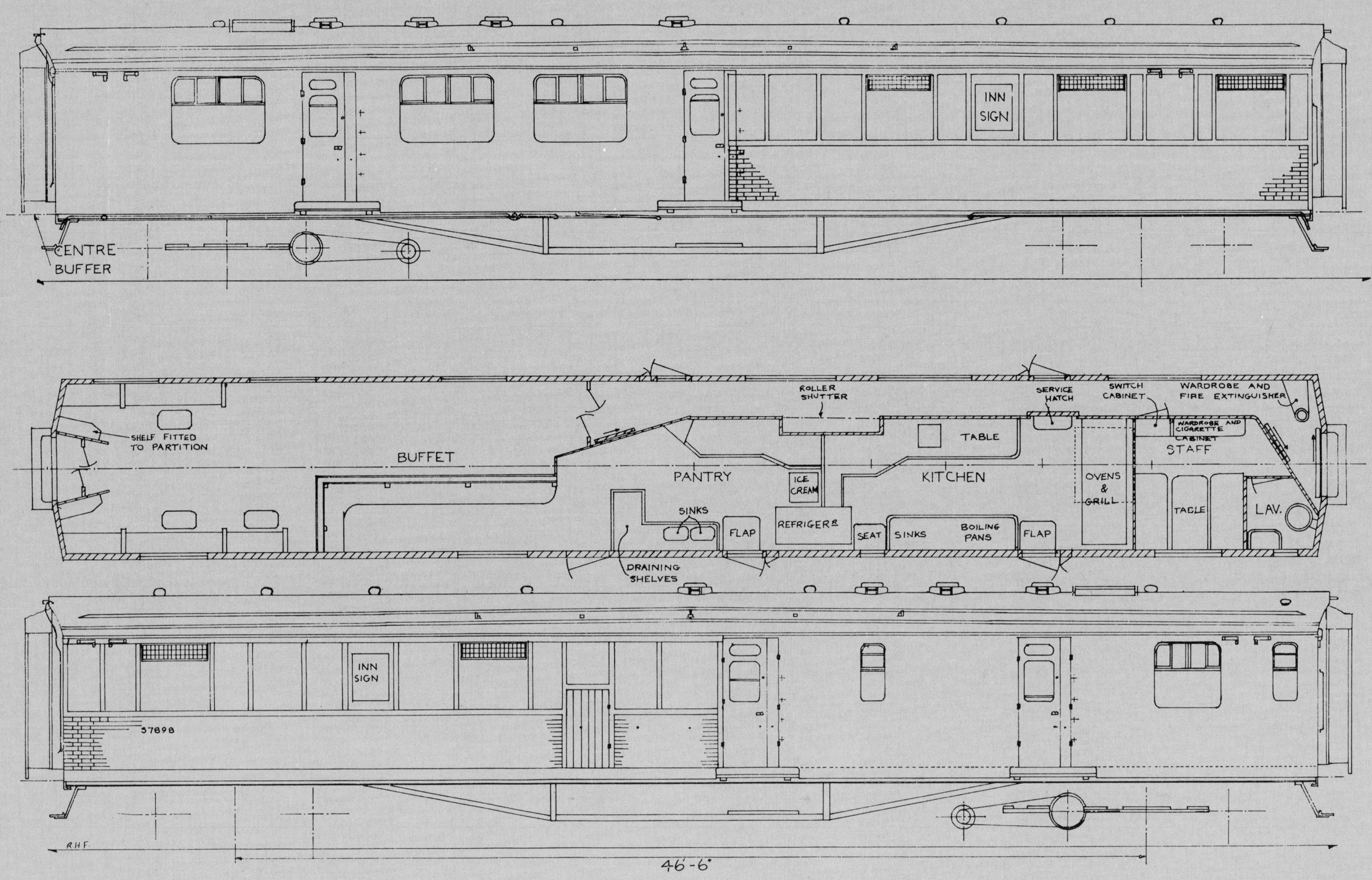

Tavern Car — 1st/3rd Restaurant Car (Tavern Trailer)

Drawing No 23

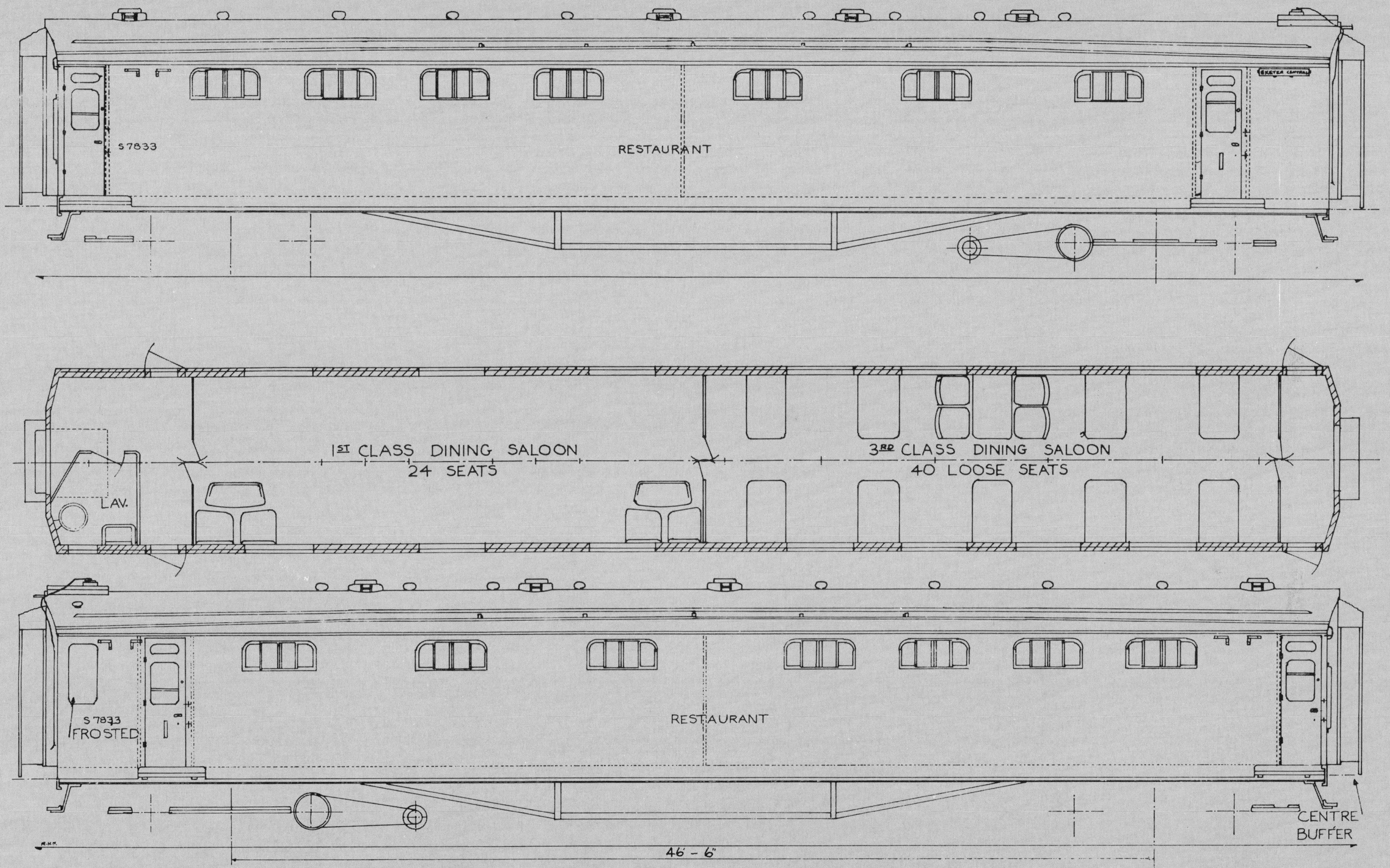

Drawing No 24

Rebuilt Tavern Cars — Composite Dining Saloon

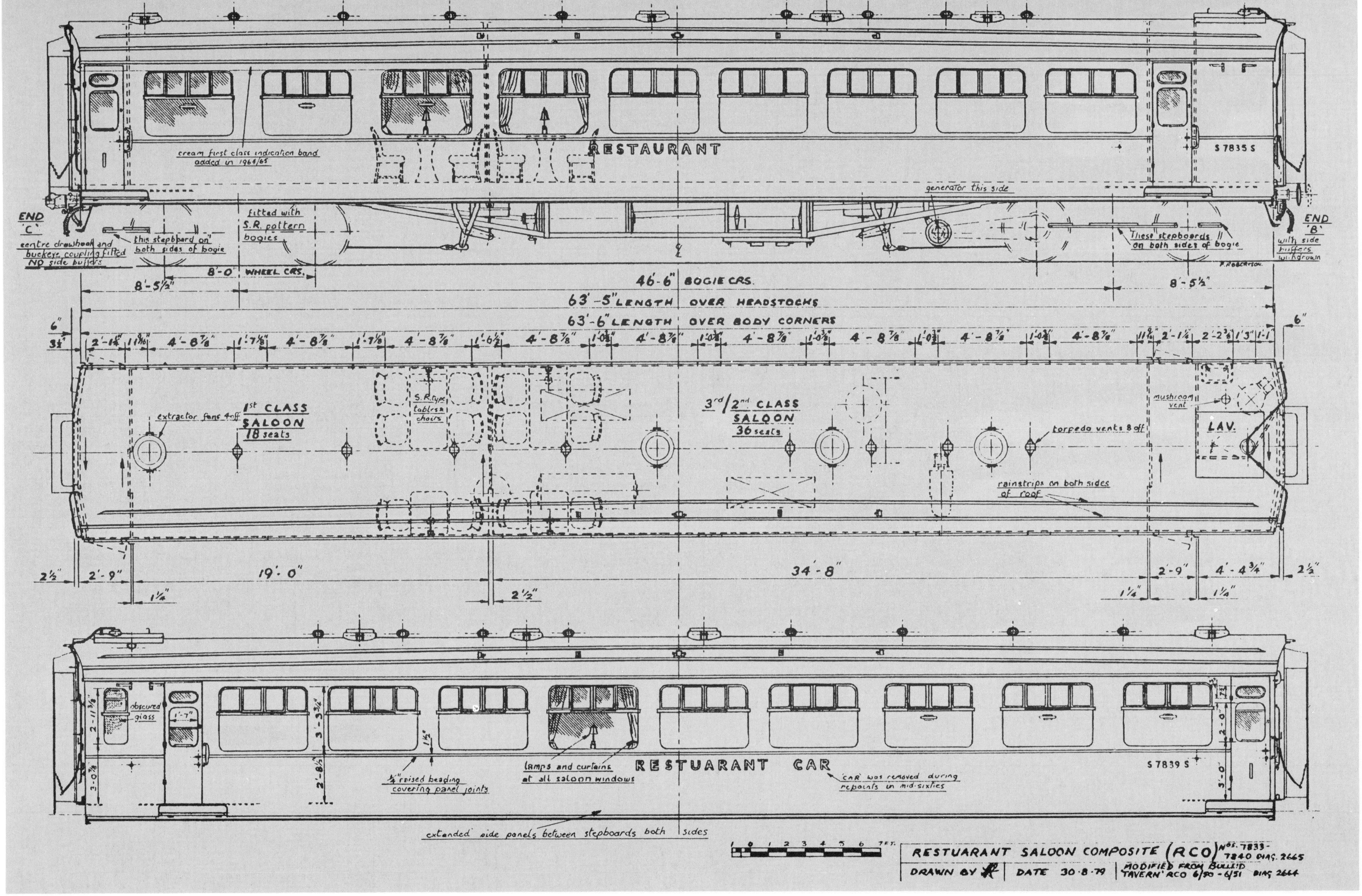

Buffet Kitchen Car

Drawing No 25

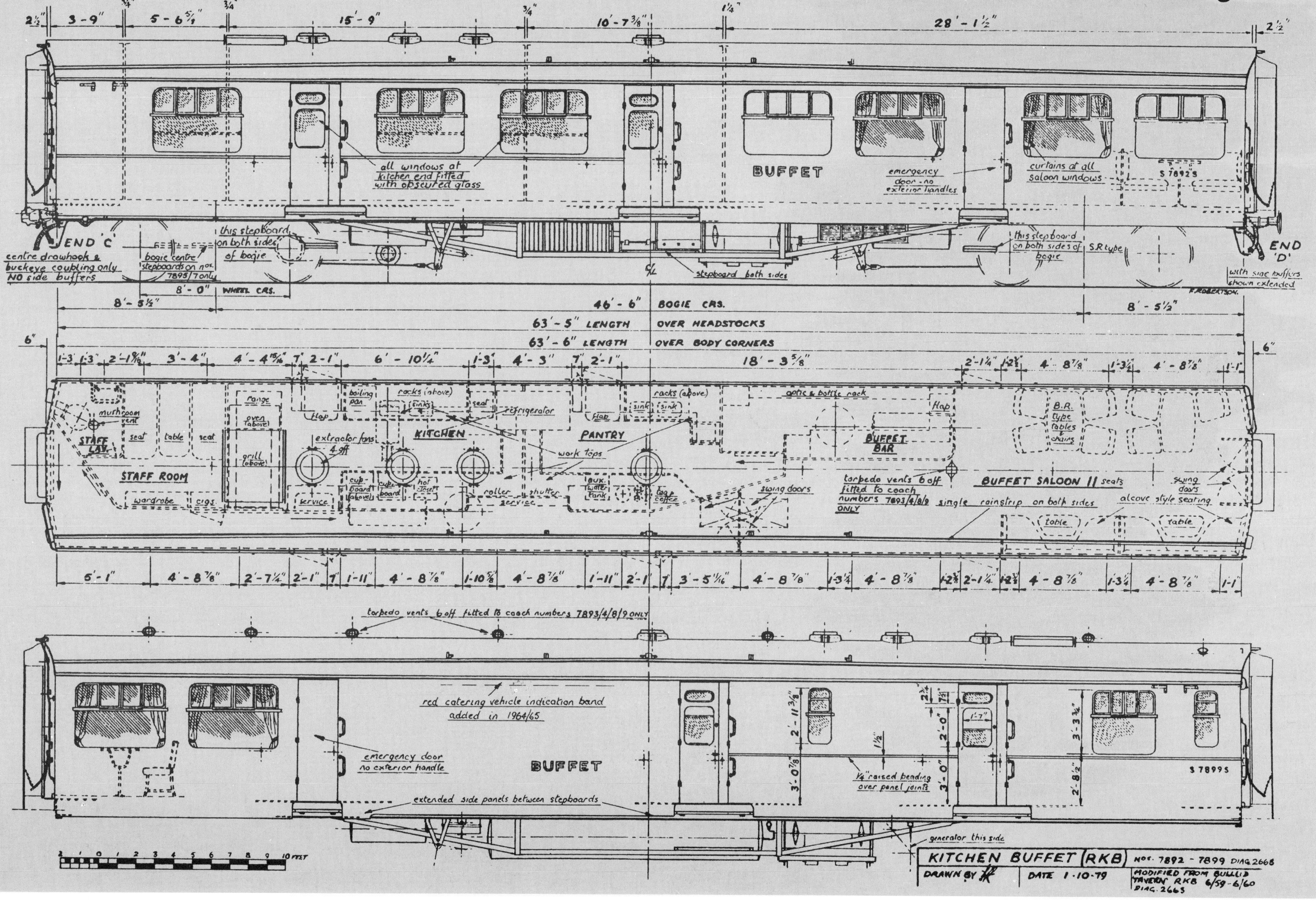

The 4SUB Electric Units

Introduction

At the Annual General Meeting of the Southern Railway in February 1939, the Chairman referred to the growth of rush hour traffic (now called commuter traffic) and announced that they were designing new six-aside seating suburban electric trains which would have curved and welded sides.

The first of the new trains (No 4101) did not appear until 1941 and was the first new suburban stock built since 1925. It was also the first four-coach electric suburban unit, for up to that time all the electric unit were of three-coaches which, for the rush hours, were joined together with two trailer coaches in between. This persisted for over 20 years in spite of operating difficulties with remarshalling the units and their trailers at least twice a day. The new trains were also the first electric suburban units to utilise a numerical headcode instead of the letters previously used.

Thus began the series known as 4SUB, later to become BR Class 405/1. They were sometimes known as the 1936 stock because they were fitted with the 275hp English Electric (Type EE339) traction motors and the electro-pneumatic control gear, the same as used on the 2BIL semi-fast stock which was introduced in 1936 for the the Waterloo-Portsmouth electrification. They were also fitted with Westinghouse air brakes and screw couplings on the outer ends. The standard Southern metal stencil headcode plates were supplied which were fitted in front of a white glass and electrically illuminated at night. However, as the 4SUB units were not fitted with emergency batteries, they all had to have rear oil lamps. The maximum speed of the units was 70mph. Jumper cables were placed below the cab windows and brake cables at buffer beam level.

The external appearance of the new trains was quite revolutionary for the convex body design fitted the SR loading gauge with the flush sides brought up to the main roof panel instead of stopping at the cant rail. It is claimed that this design of all steel construction was stronger and more attractive as well as being easier to construct and maintain than the conventional design. Likewise all the interior fittings were designed for easy assembly and maintenance.

The new design was enhanced by large windows with a 'toplight' above the droplight in the door as an aid for standing passengers, thus they were sometimes called 'glasshouses' by the staff, but this soon gave way to the nickname 'Queen of Sheba's' (who is purported to have had a very great train!) and this was abbreviated to 'Queens' or 'Sheba's'.

The underframe of 61ft 11$\frac{1}{2}$in were constructed at Lancing Works, while the bodies were built at Eastleigh. The motor coaches had an overall length of 62ft 6in and the trailer coaches 62ft (both measurements excluding buffers). The total length of a 4SUB is 257ft 4$\frac{1}{2}$in, the width is 9ft 3in, while the weight is 144ton unladen.

Due to wartime restrictions the second unit, No 4102, did not appear until late 1944, by which time first class travel had been abolished for all suburban routes. These first two units worked the Victoria-Orpington services until mid-1945. The remainder of the eight units were completed by April 1945 and the next batch were built a year later, thereafter the 4SUBs were produced in quantity. The variations are given for the various units in dealing with the particular drawings. As the trailer units could be completed quicker than the motor coaches, due to delays with control gear etc, they were used to augment the existing fleet of three-coach units until sufficient numbers of the motor coaches could be built.

◀ Unit No 4102 on a Hampton Court-Waterloo service at Raynes Park in May 1960 and still in Southern green.
S. W. Stevens-Stratten

▲ Unit No 4107 with yellow ends on Chessington North to Waterloo train in March 1970 passing Wimbledon.
J. H. Cooper-Smith

▲ Unit No 4101 stabled at Shepperton. *A. McIntyre*

Unit Nos 4101-4110 — Drawing Nos 26-29

The first of the 4SUBs with all steel curved sides, large windows, domed steel ends to the roof over the drivers cab, which was inset from the curved sides. The remainder of the roof, and those on the trailer coaches was wood planking covered with canvas. The frontal appearance was similar to the 2HAL units introduced for the electrification to the Medway towns.

The complete unit was composed of a Motor Brake third (to become a second) with nine compartments seating 108 with a small guard's compartment; an 11 compartment trailer third; a 10 compartment trailer composite (two 3rds, six 1sts and two 3rds); and another identical nine compartment Motor Brake third.

Close-up of front end of 4SUB No 4101 in August 1972. *J. Scrace*

The total seating was 456 (60 at 1st and 396 at 3rd). Due to the close proximity of the seats in every compartment they became known as 'knee knockers' and there was virtually no room to stand.

Almost immediately after the introduction of unit No 4101 at the end of 1941 the first class accommodation for suburban trains was abolished. Thus when the second unit (No 4102) was put into service in December 1944, the composite vehicle, although to the same dimensions had the third class six-aside seating and therefore the total seating was 468 and remained thus for the other units in this series.

Numbers of coaches as originally in service:

Motor Brake Third	10941-10960
Trailer Third	10419-10428
Trailer Composite	11471-11480

Unit No 4101 entered service late in 1941, No 4102 in December 1944 and Nos 4103-4110 between January and April 1945. All were withdrawn in 1971 but Motor Coach of unit No 4103 was written off in a collision at Norwood Junction in 1968 and replaced by 2HAL coach No 2644.

Unit Nos 4111-4120 — Drawing Nos 30-36

Following complaints of cramped conditions in the motor brake coaches of the first batch of units (Nos 4101-4110) the compartments were made wider (6ft 1½in) and reduced to eight in number as against nine of the original design. Another immediately recognisable feaure is the change in the front end design, for no longer is the roof domed over the driver's cab, but the roof line is carried to the extremity of the front end and is all steel. Another change is that the driver's cab is no longer inset, but follows the contour of the coach side. The trailer coaches are of 10 and 9 compartments making a total seating capacity of 420.

These units which entered service in 1946 formed the basis for the huge fleet of 4SUB electric units of the Southern Region of BR.

Numbers of coaches as originally in service:

Motor Brake Third	10961-10980
Trailer Third	10429-10438
Trailer Composite	11481-11490

One of the second batch of 4SUBs. Unit No 4115 leaving Waterloo in Southern livery in July 1949. *C. C. B. Herbert*

One of the same batch but in June 1950 and painted with BR numbering with the 'S' prefix. *C. C. B. Herbert*

Front view of 4SUB, now Class 405, showing the various items of detail. (1) Control jumper, (2) Power jumper socket, (3 and 4) Lighting control jumpers, (5) Power jumper, (6) Control jumper socket, (7) Main reservoir pipe, (8) Brake pipe, (9) Draw hook, (10) Stencil headcode — newer SR units now have roller blind headcodes. *Colin Marsden*

Unit Nos 4121-4130 — Drawing Nos 30-36

These units were also built in 1946 and were virtually identical to Nos 4111-4120 in external appearance but only in one of the trailer coaches were separate compartments retained. This was the beginning of the open saloon type of coach for Southern Region suburban travel which has continued to this day. The Motor Brake Seconds (power cars) comprised of two four-bay sections having two and three seats with a central gangway between them (except, of course, those against the partitions which were of the usual six-aside seating). One trailer had three, four and three seating bays, while the remaining trailer had the conventional nine compartments (as in units Nos 4111-4120). The open type coach gave greater standing accommodation for rush hour traffic and in the slack periods was a prevention against 'mugging' and other attacks which had sometimes been made on a single occupant of a compartment.

The seating was reduced to 382 (84 in each of the Motor Brake Seconds. 106 in the Open Trailer, and 108 in the Compartment Trailer).

The numbers of coaches in the unit as originally in service:

Motor Brake Second	10981-11000
Trailer Open Second	10439-10448
Trailer Second (Compartment)	11491-11500

Although not affecting the external appearance, unit No 4130 was fitted with a new self ventilating, totally enclosed 185hp (later 250hp) English Electric type 507 motor, which was 6ton lighter than the previous motors. However, this was replaced eight years later with a conventional motor. The weight on unit No 4130 as built was 142ton.

Units Nos 4277-4299, 4355-4387, 4601-4607, 4621-4754 — Drawing Nos 30-36

These units completed in late 1948 to early 1951 are unchanged externally from the previous units but the interiors of the coaches, except for one trailer which has compartments, now have full length open saloons as against the sectionalised ones. Armrests were given to the seats adjoining the open gangway. However, both trailers in unit Nos 4601-4607 had compartments. Units Nos 4694-4700, 4718, 4721 and 4736 all had roller blind headcodes from inception in place of the standard metal headcode stencils plates.

There has been a considerable amount of swapping not only of trailer coaches (but also power cars) in all these units and some were taken from the older 3SUB units which had used an 'Augmentation trailer'. Some of the units were fitted with the lightweight motor.

A close-up of the front showing twin tone horns on roof and other detail. *R. I. Wallace*

Waterloo to Dorking train at Wimbledon in September 1980. *Colin Marsden*

A view of the complete roof of the 4SUB unit. An up train in Clapham Cutting in August 1973. *Brian Morrison*

The shoe beam and shoe for current collection (750V dc) on a 4SUB unit. Bogie detail can also be seen. The shoe fuse box is under the guard's door. *Colin Marsden*

Close-up view showing door hinges, door and grab handles. *Ian Allan Library*

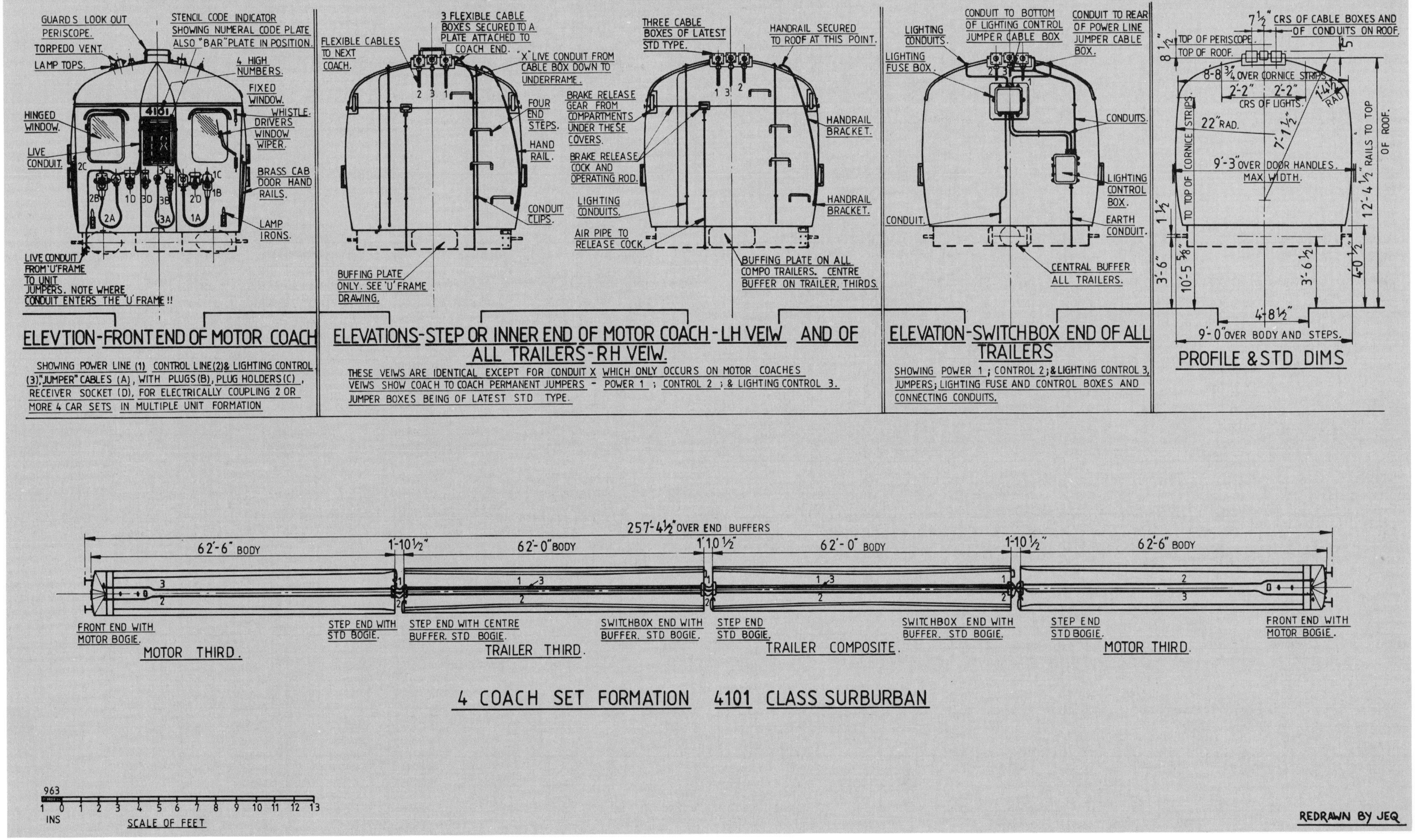
GUARDS LOOK OUT PERISCOPE.
STENCIL CODE INDICATOR SHOWING NUMERAL CODE PLATE ALSO "BAR" PLATE IN POSITION.
TORPEDO VENT.
LAMP TOPS.
4 HIGH NUMBERS.
FIXED WINDOW.
WHISTLE.
HINGED WINDOW.
DRIVERS WINDOW WIPER.
LIVE CONDUIT.
BRASS CAB DOOR HAND RAILS.
LAMP IRONS.
LIVE CONDUIT FROM 'U' FRAME TO UNIT JUMPERS. NOTE WHERE CONDUIT ENTERS THE 'U' FRAME !!
ELEVTION-FRONT END OF MOTOR COACH
SHOWING POWER LINE (1) CONTROL LINE (2) & LIGHTING CONTROL (3) "JUMPER" CABLES (A), WITH PLUGS (B), PLUG HOLDERS (C), RECEIVER SOCKET (D), FOR ELECTRICALLY COUPLING 2 OR MORE 4 CAR SETS IN MULTIPLE UNIT FORMATION
FLEXIBLE CABLES TO NEXT COACH.
3 FLEXIBLE CABLE BOXES SECURED TO A PLATE ATTACHED TO COACH END.
"X" LIVE CONDUIT FROM CABLE BOX DOWN TO UNDERFRAME.
FOUR END STEPS.
HAND RAIL.
CONDUIT CLIPS.
BUFFING PLATE ONLY. SEE 'U' FRAME DRAWING.
THREE CABLE BOXES OF LATEST STD TYPE.
HANDRAIL SECURED TO ROOF AT THIS POINT.
BRAKE RELEASE GEAR FROM COMPARTMENTS UNDER THESE COVERS.
BRAKE RELEASE COCK AND OPERATING ROD.
LIGHTING CONDUITS.
AIR PIPE TO RELEASE COCK.
HANDRAIL BRACKET.
HANDRAIL BRACKET.
BUFFING PLATE ON ALL COMPO TRAILERS. CENTRE BUFFER ON TRAILER. THIRDS.
ELEVATIONS-STEP OR INNER END OF MOTOR COACH - LH VEIW AND OF ALL TRAILERS - RH VEIW.
THESE VEIWS ARE IDENTICAL EXCEPT FOR CONDUIT X WHICH ONLY OCCURS ON MOTOR COACHES VEIWS SHOW COACH TO COACH PERMANENT JUMPERS - POWER 1 ; CONTROL 2 ; & LIGHTING CONTROL 3. JUMPER BOXES BEING OF LATEST STD TYPE.
LIGHTING CONDUITS.
CONDUIT TO BOTTOM OF LIGHTING CONTROL JUMPER CABLE BOX
CONDUIT TO REAR OF POWER LINE JUMPER CABLE BOX.
LIGHTING FUSE BOX.
CONDUITS.
LIGHTING CONTROL BOX.
EARTH CONDUIT.
CONDUIT.
CENTRAL BUFFER ALL TRAILERS.
ELEVATION-SWITCHBOX END OF ALL TRAILERS
SHOWING POWER 1 ; CONTROL 2 ; & LIGHTING CONTROL 3, JUMPERS; LIGHTING FUSE AND CONTROL BOXES AND CONNECTING CONDUITS.
7½" CRS OF CABLE BOXES AND OF CONDUITS ON ROOF.
TOP OF PERISCOPE.
TOP OF ROOF.
8-8¾ OVER CORNICE STRIPS
2'-2" 2'-2" CRS OF LIGHTS.
1'-4½" RAD.
22" RAD.
7'-1½"
9'-3" OVER DOOR HANDLES. MAX WIDTH.
TO TOP OF CORNICE STRIPS.
12'-4½" RAILS TO TOP OF ROOF.
10'-5⅝"
3'-6"
3'-6½"
4'-0½"
4'-8½"
9'-0" OVER BODY AND STEPS.
PROFILE & STD DIMS
257'-4½" OVER END BUFFERS
62'-6" BODY
1'-10½"
62'-0" BODY
1'10½"
62'-0" BODY
1'-10½"
62'-6" BODY
FRONT END WITH MOTOR BOGIE.
MOTOR THIRD.
STEP END WITH STD BOGIE.
STEP END WITH CENTRE BUFFER. STD BOGIE.
TRAILER THIRD.
SWITCHBOX END WITH BUFFER. STD BOGIE.
STEP END STD BOGIE.
TRAILER COMPOSITE.
SWITCHBOX END WITH BUFFER. STD BOGIE.
STEP END STD BOGIE.
MOTOR THIRD.
FRONT END WITH MOTOR BOGIE.
4 COACH SET FORMATION 4101 CLASS SURBURBAN
963
1 0 1 2 3 4 5 6 7 8 9 10 11 12 13
INS
SCALE OF FEET
REDRAWN BY JEQ

4SUB

Drawing No 27

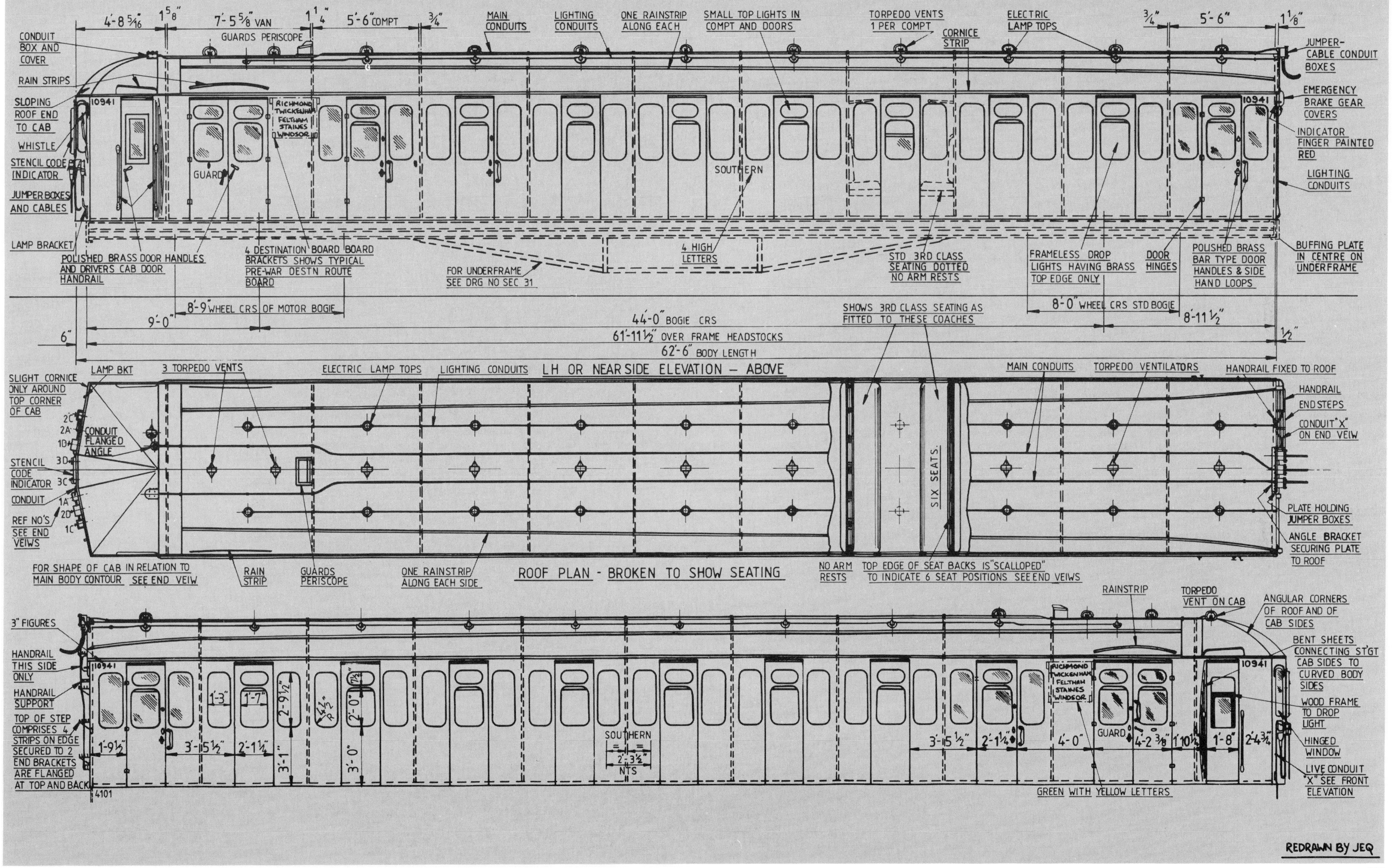

Drawing No 28

4SUB

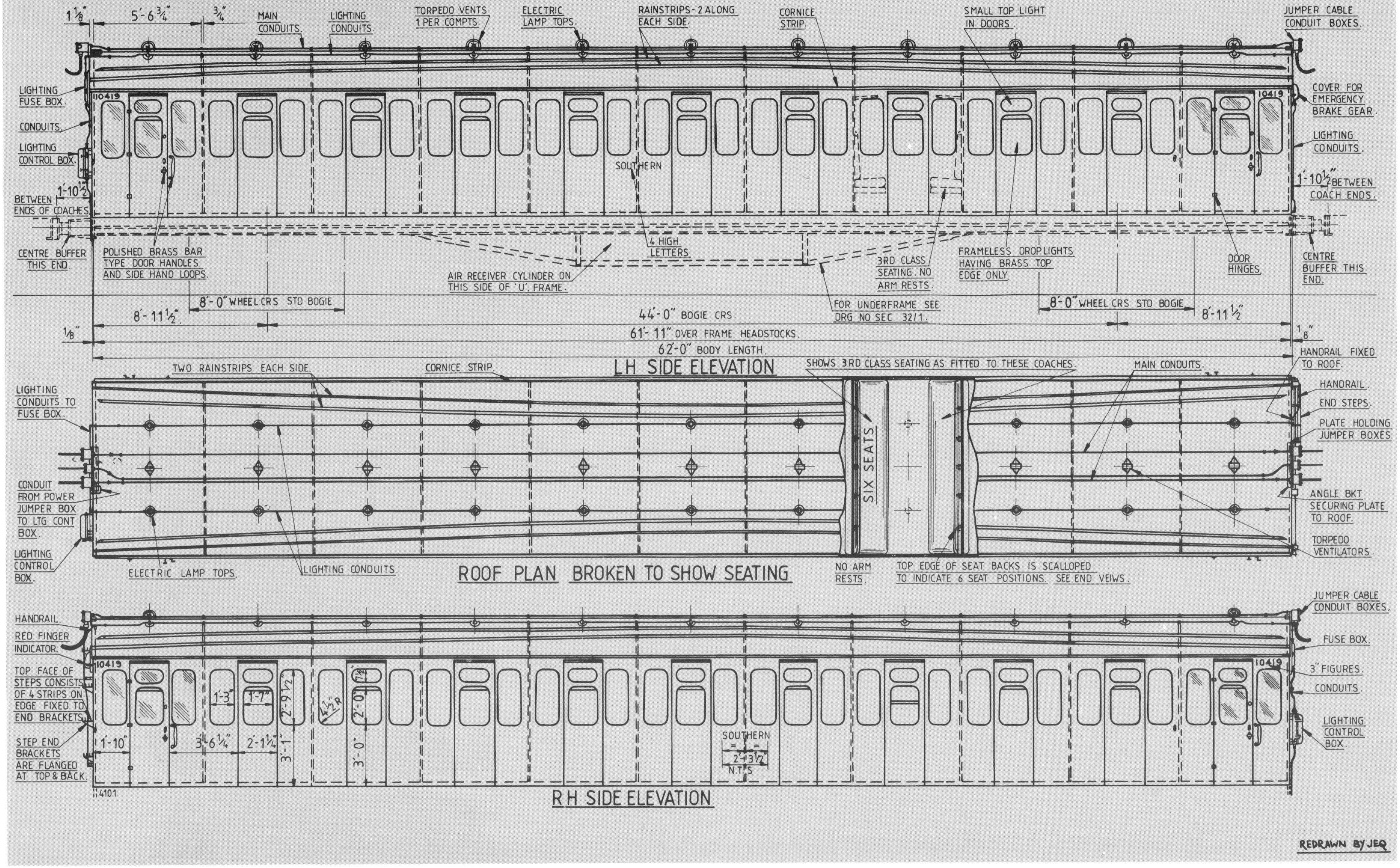

Drawing No 29

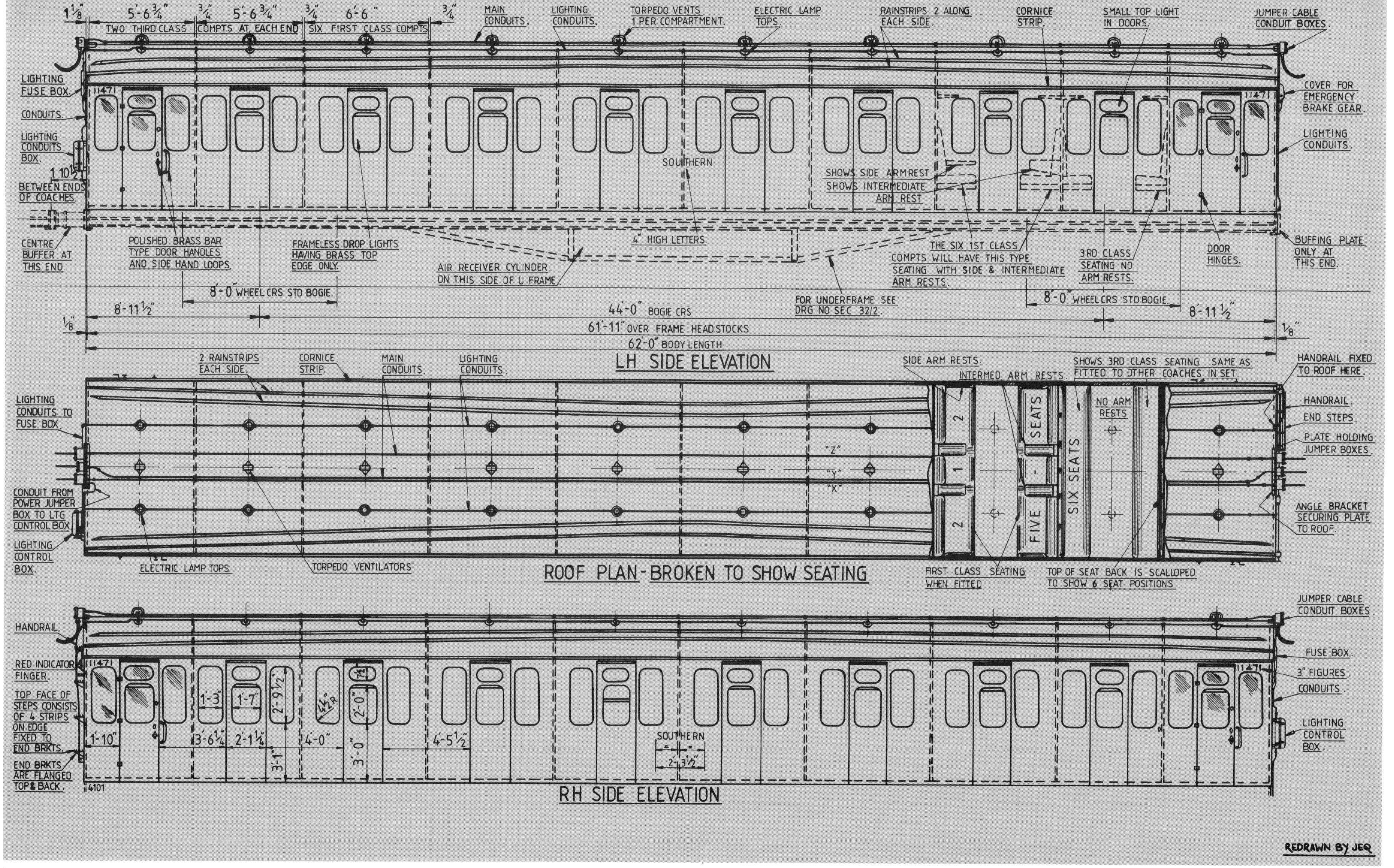

Drawing No 30

4SUB

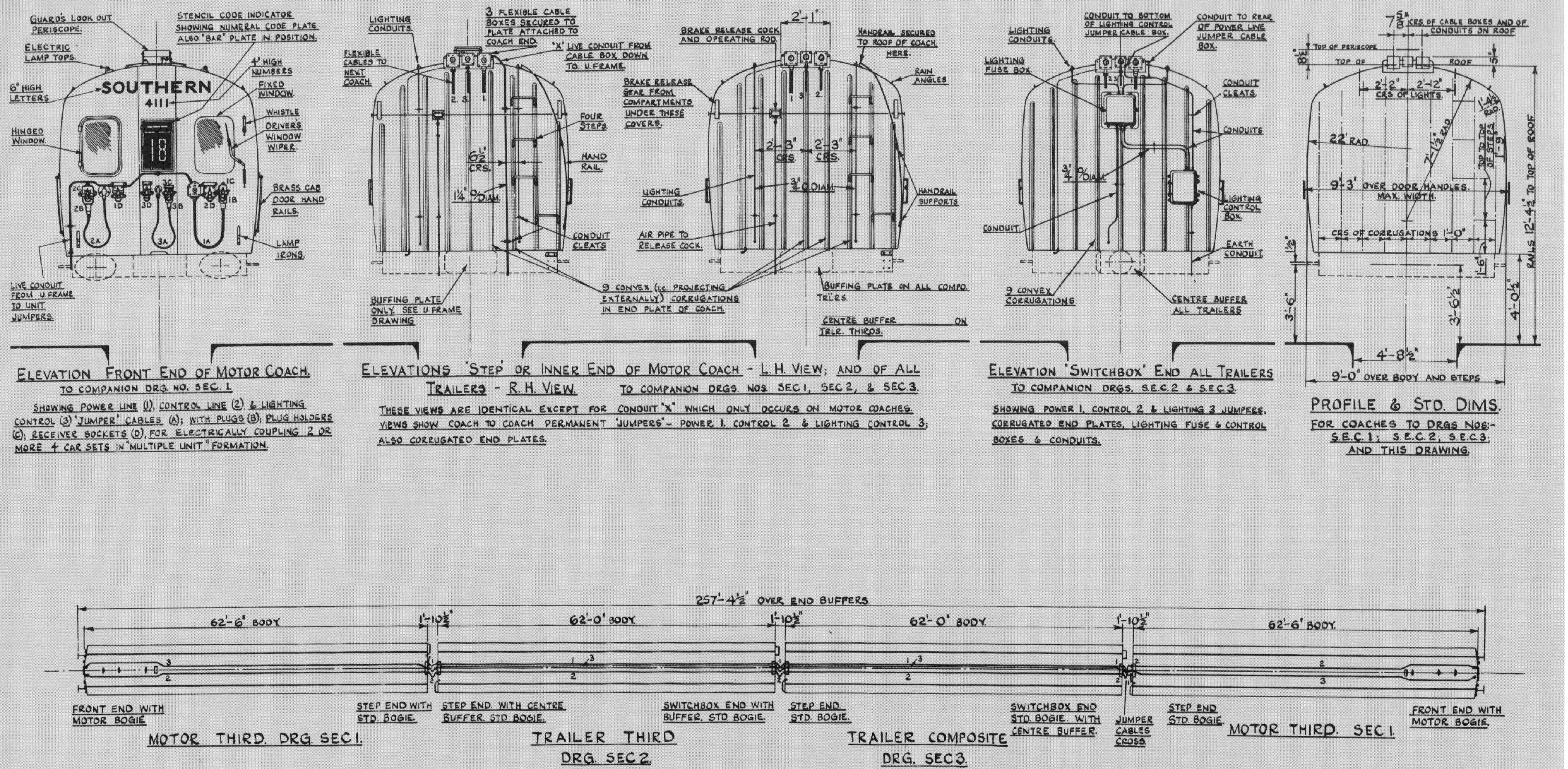

FOUR COACH SET FORMATION OF SUBURBAN STOCK 1946 & LATER. 4111 & 4121 SERIES SETS. (ALSO 4364-77)

Drawing No 31

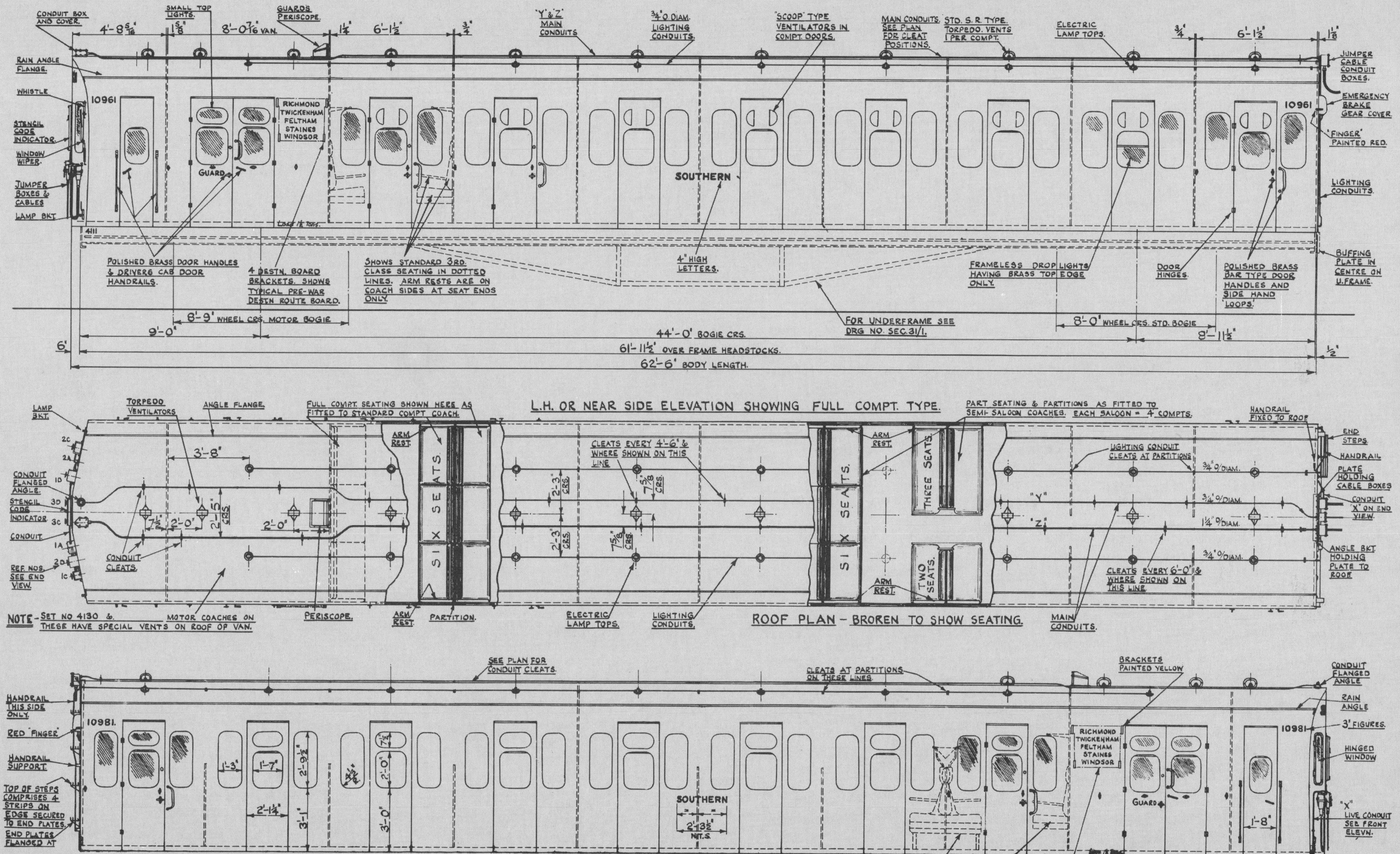

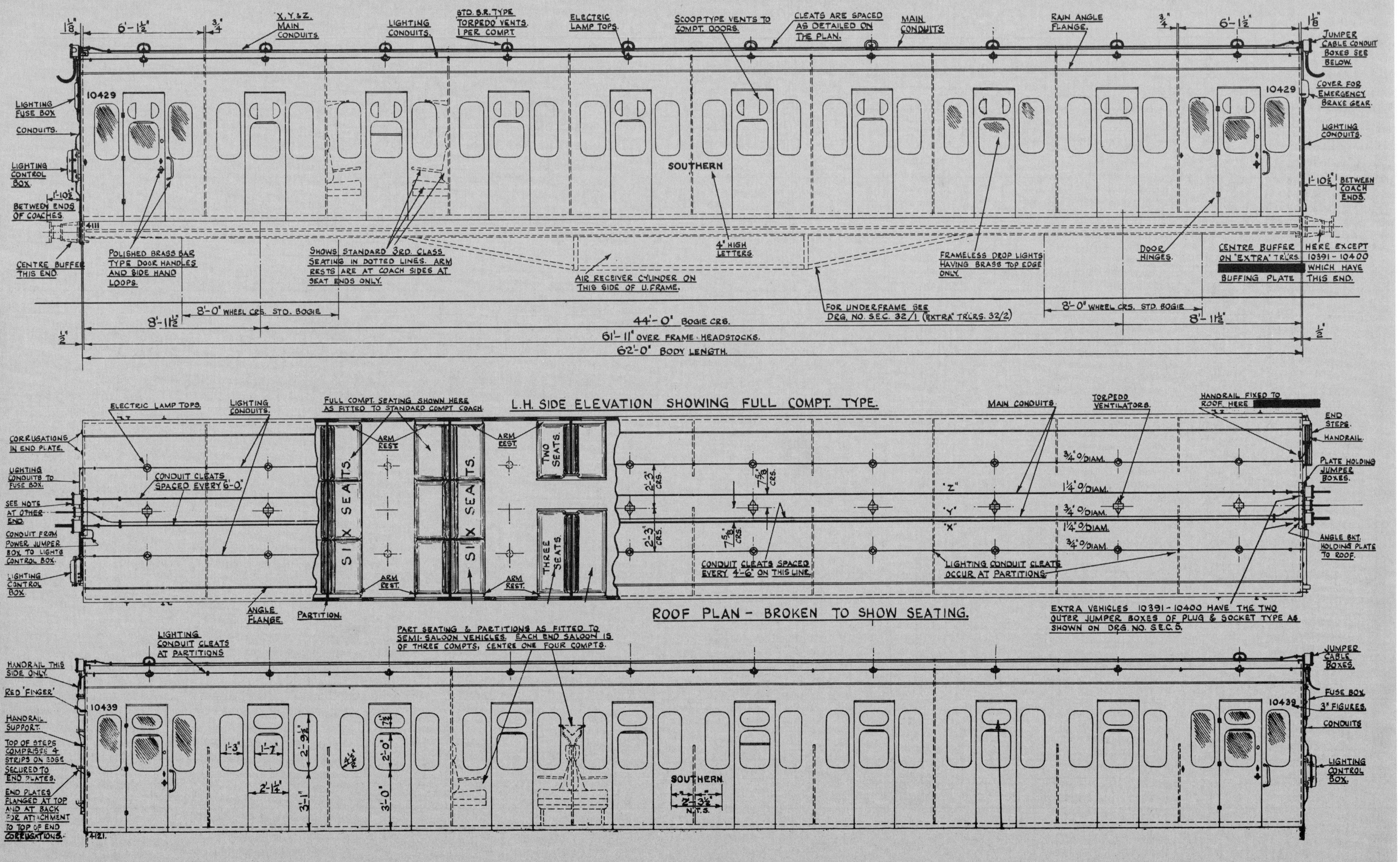

X, Y & Z. MAIN CONDUITS
LIGHTING CONDUITS.
STD. S.R. TYPE TORPEDO VENTS. 1 PER COMPT.
ELECTRIC LAMP TOPS.
SCOOP TYPE VENTS TO COMPT. DOORS.
CLEATS ARE SPACED AS DETAILED ON THE PLAN.
MAIN CONDUITS
RAIN ANGLE FLANGE.
JUMPER CABLE CONDUIT BOXES SEE BELOW.
COVER FOR EMERGENCY BRAKE GEAR.
LIGHTING CONDUITS.
1'-10½" BETWEEN COACH ENDS.
LIGHTING FUSE BOX
CONDUITS.
LIGHTING CONTROL BOX.
1'-10½" BETWEEN ENDS OF COACHES.
CENTRE BUFFER THIS END.
10429
SOUTHERN
POLISHED BRASS BAR TYPE DOOR HANDLES AND SIDE HAND LOOPS.
SHOWS STANDARD 3RD CLASS SEATING IN DOTTED LINES. ARM RESTS ARE AT COACH SIDES AT SEAT ENDS ONLY.
4" HIGH LETTERS.
AIR RECEIVER CYLINDER ON THIS SIDE OF U.FRAME.
FRAMELESS DROP LIGHTS HAVING BRASS TOP EDGE ONLY.
DOOR HINGES.
CENTRE BUFFER HERE EXCEPT ON 'EXTRA' TR'LRS. 10391-10400 [redacted] WHICH HAVE BUFFING PLATE THIS END.
FOR UNDERFRAME SEE DRG. NO. SEC. 32/1 (EXTRA TR'LRS. 32/2)
8'-0" WHEEL CRS. STD. BOGIE
8'-11½"
44'-0" BOGIE CRS.
61'-11" OVER FRAME HEADSTOCKS.
62'-0" BODY LENGTH.
L.H. SIDE ELEVATION SHOWING FULL COMPT. TYPE.
ELECTRIC LAMP TOPS.
LIGHTING CONDUITS.
FULL COMPT. SEATING SHOWN HERE AS FITTED TO STANDARD COMPT COACH.
MAIN CONDUITS
TORPEDO VENTILATORS.
HANDRAIL FIXED TO ROOF HERE [redacted]
END STEPS.
HANDRAIL.
PLATE HOLDING JUMPER BOXES.
ANGLE BKT. HOLDING PLATE TO ROOF.
CORRUGATIONS IN END PLATE.
LIGHTING CONDUITS TO FUSE BOX.
CONDUIT CLEATS SPACED EVERY 6'-0"
SEE NOTES AT OTHER END.
CONDUIT FROM POWER JUMPER BOX TO LIGHTS CONTROL BOX.
LIGHTING CONTROL BOX.
ARM REST.
SIX SEATS.
TWO SEATS.
THREE SEATS.
¾" O/DIAM.
1¼" O/DIAM.
"Z"
"Y"
"X"
CONDUIT CLEATS SPACED EVERY 4'-6" ON THIS LINE.
LIGHTING CONDUIT CLEATS OCCUR AT PARTITIONS.
ANGLE FLANGE.
PARTITION.
ROOF PLAN - BROKEN TO SHOW SEATING.
EXTRA VEHICLES 10391-10400 HAVE THE TWO OUTER JUMPER BOXES OF PLUG & SOCKET TYPE AS SHOWN ON DRG. NO. SEC.5.
LIGHTING CONDUIT CLEATS AT PARTITIONS.
PART SEATING & PARTITIONS AS FITTED TO SEMI-SALOON VEHICLES. EACH END SALOON IS OF THREE COMPTS, CENTRE ONE FOUR COMPTS.
HANDRAIL THIS SIDE ONLY.
'RED FINGER'
HANDRAIL SUPPORT.
TOP OF STEPS COMPRISES 4 STRIPS ON EDGE SECURED TO END PLATES.
END PLATES FLANGED AT TOP AND AT BACK FOR ATTACHMENT TO TOP OF END CORRUGATIONS.
10439
JUMPER CABLE BOXES.
FUSE BOX.
3" FIGURES.
CONDUITS.
LIGHTING CONTROL BOX.
N.T.S.

Drawing No 33

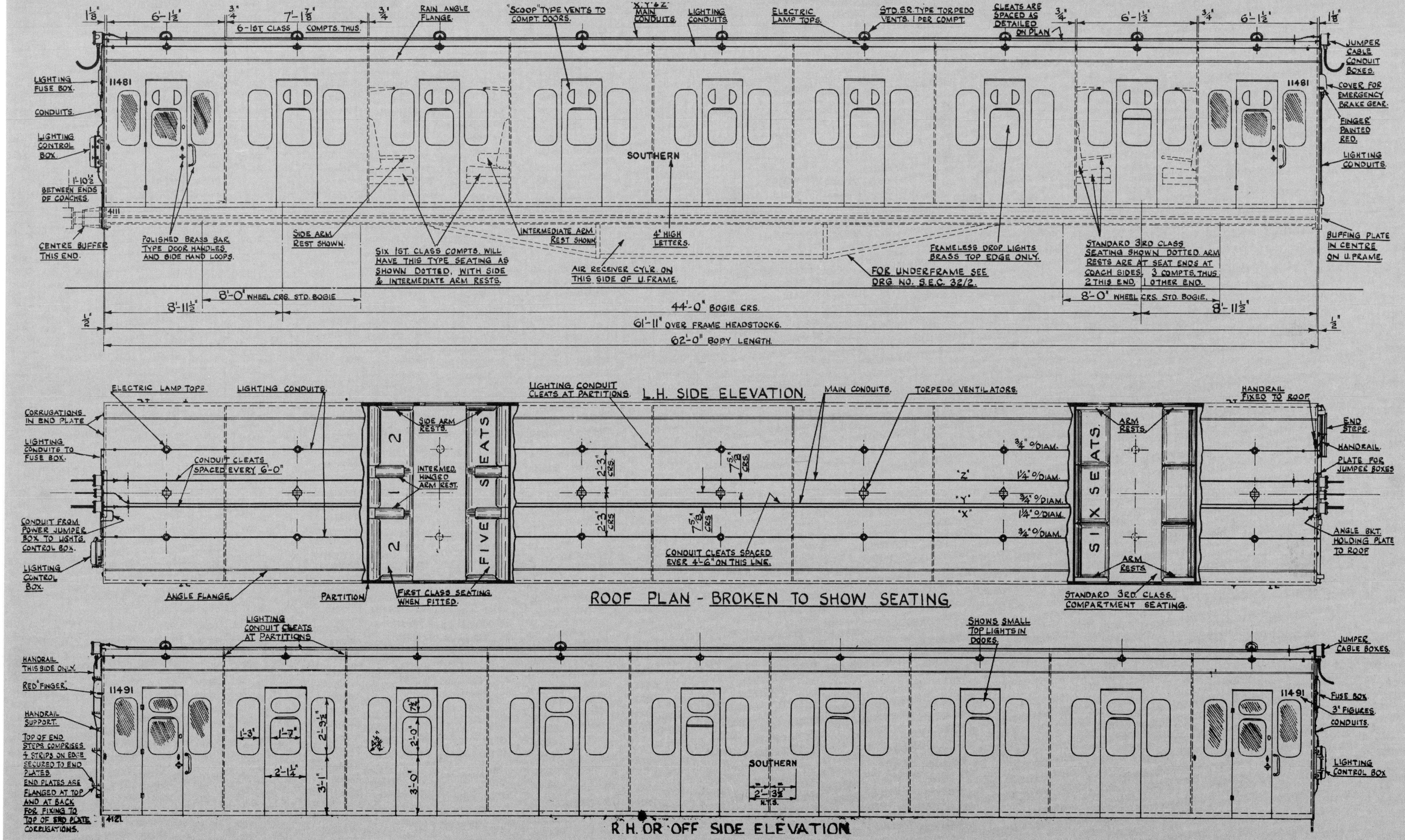

Drawing No 34

4SUB

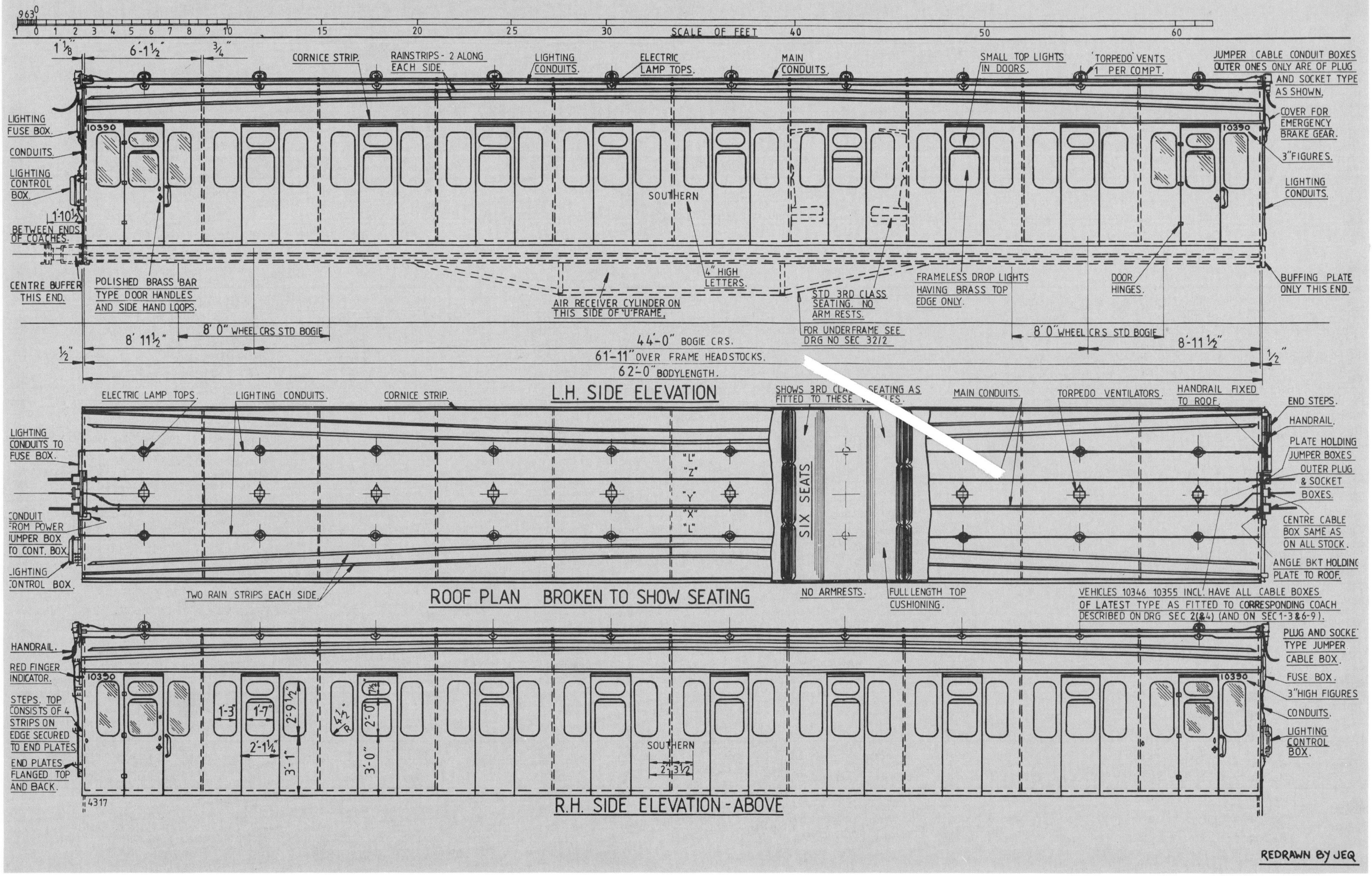

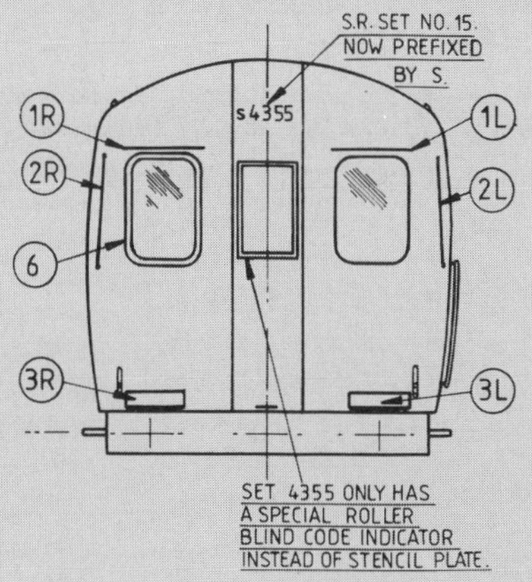

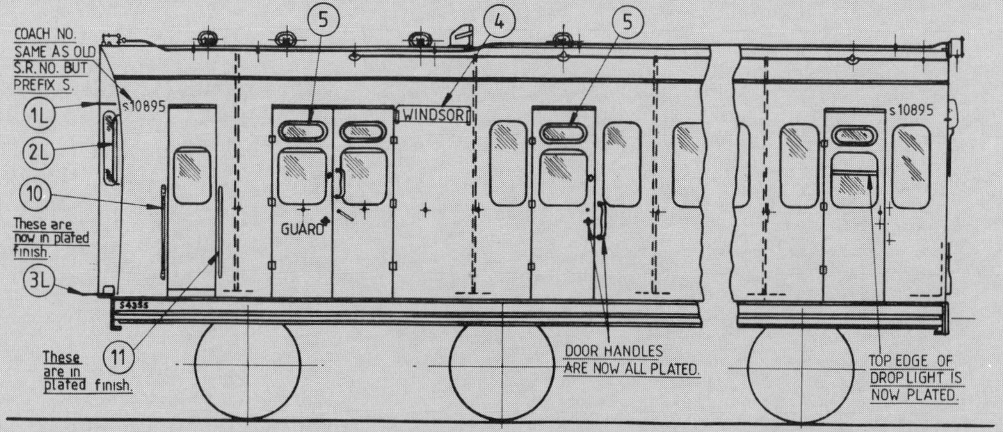

FRONT END OF MOTOR COACH.

INNER END.

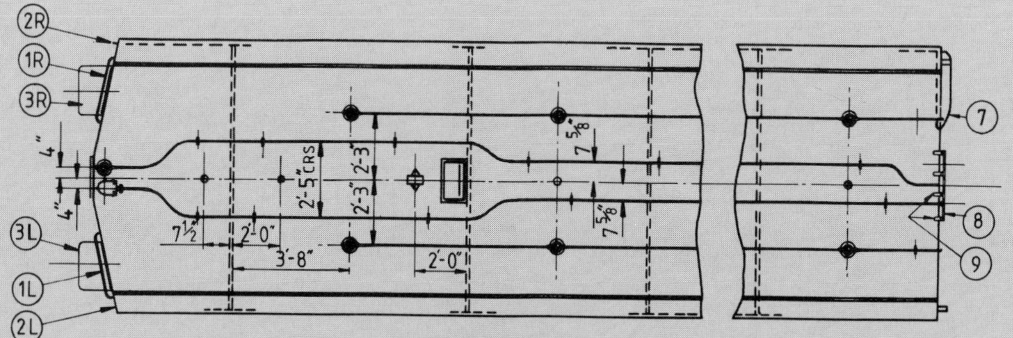

PLAN OF ABOVE.

1R and 2R Handrails 3R step plate	Fitted only to sets Nos 4355-4387 and 4277-4299.
1L, 2L and 3L	Fitted only to sets Nos 4355-4366 and 4277-4299.

4 — Small dest'n board and 2 bkts only (and *not* 4 bkts as on sets 4111-4120).
5 — Combined vent and sunk top light as now fitted to all doors (except cab).
6 — Window fixed on sets 4355-4387 and 4277-4299.
7 — Handrail as before but note where now fixed to roof.
8 — Std plate for securing three jumper boxes to coach.
9 — 4 angle bkts fixing 8 to roof.
10 — Std handrail as on 4111-4120 but now plated (on first few only).
11 — New plated handrails as fitted to all sets listed here (except perhaps the first few).

REDRAWN BY JEQ

Drawing No 36

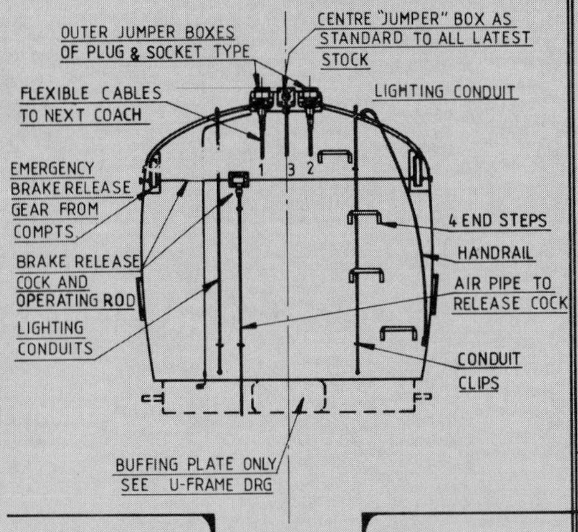

ELEVATION OF STEP END OF COACH
TO COMPANION DRG SEC 5
SHOWS "JUMPERS" - POWER 1; CONTROL 2; BOTH OF PLUG & SOCKET TYPES; & LIGHTING CONTROL 3 OF STANDARD TYPE. FIRST 10 HAVE ALL JUMPERS OF LATEST STD TYPE SEE ⟶

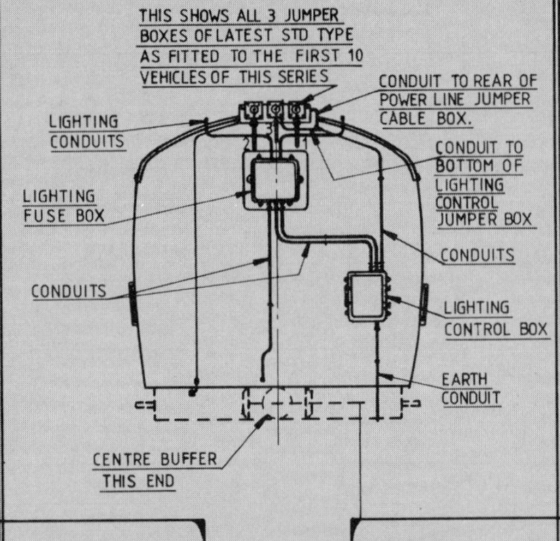

ELEVATION OF SWITCHBOX END
TO COMPANION DRG SEC 5
SHOWS "JUMPERS" POWER 1; CONTROL 2; LIGHTING CONT 3. ALL OF LATEST TYPE AS ON FIRST 10 COACHES. ALSO LIGHTING CONTROL AND FUSE BOXES & CONDUITS.

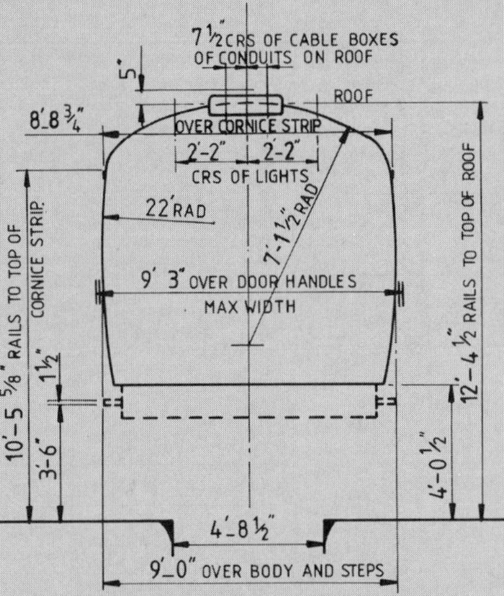

PROFILE & STD DIMENSIONS
FOR COACH TO DRGS SEC. 5 & 6. ALSO SAME FOR COACHES TO DRGS SEC 7, 8, 9, & 10.

COACH NO	NOTES	SET NO 4300	SET NO 4326	COACH NO	NOTES	SET NO 4300	SET NO 4326
10346			4329	10375		4322	
7			43	6		13	
8	HAVE		32	7		23	
9	ALL		46	8		12	
10350	LATEST		54	9		11	
1	STD		28	10380		08	
2	JUMPER		39	1		02	
3	BOXES		62	2		05	
4			41	3		01	
5		4319		4		4300	
6	ALL		34	5		21	
7	THE	15		6		24	
8	REST		43	7		20	
9	HAVE		39	8		06	
10360	OUTER		47	9		14	
1	PLUG &		31	10390		17	
2	SOCKET		23	ALL STEEL COACHES TO DRG'S			
3	JUMPER		63		NO SEC	2 & 4	
4	BOXES		37	10391 *	PLUG &		4335
5			36	2 *	SOCKET		45
6		16		3 *	OUTER		48
7		18		4	JUMPER		27
8			30	5	BOXES		44
9		09		6	TO ALL		40
10370		25		7	THESE	4304	
1		03		8			33
2		10		9			51
3			50	10400			49
4		07		* THESE HAVE VENTS IN THEM			

COACH ALLOCATION — BASED ON OBSERVATION

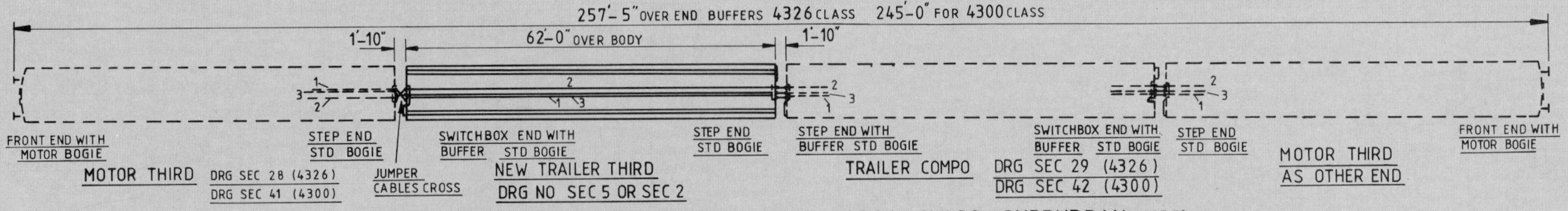

4 COACH SET FORMATION 4300 & 4326 CLASS SURBURBAN NOT TO SCALE

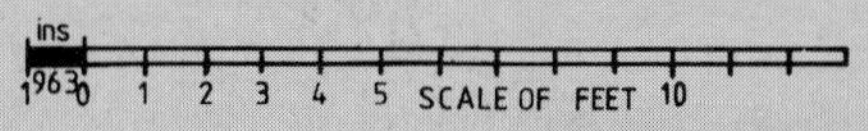

REDRAWN BY JEQ